#WHYHEWONTMARRYYOU

#WHYHEWONTMARRYYOU

AND HOW YOU CAN CHANGE THAT DYNAMIC

Gary Anthony Sturgis

Crescent City Publishing- Los Angeles, CA

#WHYHEWONTMARRYYOU

Copyright © 2018 by Gary Anthony Sturgis
All rights reserved.

Published by Gary Anthony Sturgis
Crescent City Publishing, Los Angeles, CA.

Edited by Terralyn Shelton Roach and Terri Shelton Rite, TSR Creative, Louisville, KY.
Designed by Terralyn Roach, TSR Creative, Louisville, KY.
Front cover concept by Gary Anthony Sturgis.
Front cover design by Andru Voss and Gary Anthony Sturgis.
Back cover design by Terralyn Shelton Roach, TSR Creative, Louisville, KY.
Photo by Michael Letterlough

Published in the United States of America. No portion of this book may be reproduced, stored in a retrieved system, scanned, uploaded, or shared electronically without the permission of the author/publisher, as it is unlawful piracy and theft of author's property.

ISBN 978-0-692-13432-0

*Gary Sturgis has done it again! He wears more hats than anyone I've had the honor of working with in 30 years of entertainment. He is a great actor, screenwriter, producer, director, and now, author of **#WhyHeWontMarryYou**. Gary's funny, blunt, and thought-provoking opinions are always on point. This book is guaranteed to have readers talking. I'm not one to endorse many books, but I must say this one should be on shelves with every bestseller out there.*

-Calvin Brown, Jr.
Award-winning Television Writer/Producer
Member of the Omega Psi Phi Fraternity, Inc

Gary Anthony Sturgis is an immense talent on screen, and now brings that same raw energy, deep insight, and passion to paper. With more than 25 years of marriage under his belt, Gary delivers this MASTERCLASS on how women can self-analyze and correct common mistakes when trying to get that ring. This is definitely a MUST READ for anyone seeking a lasting relationship or wishing to keep a current relationship strong. You won't want to put this book down!

-Valerie Renée
Producer/Actress

***#WhyHeWontMarryYou** is a must read for any woman wondering why he won't commit. Gary Anthony Sturgis offers eye-opening, no-holds-barred insights on relationships based on his own experiences.*

-Jean Joseph
Writer/Producer

*Gary Anthony Sturgis's new book, **#WhyHeWontMarryYou**, is truly a MASTERPIECE! As a woman married for 20 years, I agree with the reasons he gives as to why men don't ask certain women for their hand in marriage! Required reading!*

-Lee Scott-Armstrong
Actress

Gary has a gift for revealing the unapologetic, often uncomfortable truths behind male-female interaction. Now, the world will finally get to read what those in relationships wouldn't dare say out loud.

-Brad James
Actor

With **#WhyHeWontMarryYou**, *author Gary Sturgis has written the ultimate manifesto for relationships in today's internet and social-media-connected times. Gary truly keeps it real with the mindset of today's single man, as he navigates the murky waters of dating in 2018. So ladies, if you're looking to build a strong, lasting, happy relationship, READ THIS BOOK!!!*

-Greg Carter
Writer/Director/Producer

Dedicated to my mother

Sarah Sturgis

Sunrise: July 24, 1945 - Sunset: May 11, 2015

and

to all who seek marriage and eternal love

ACKNOWLEDGMENTS

I would like to first thank God for giving me breath, talent, and the insight to write this book. He is always first. The Alpha and the Omega.

I would like to also thank my wife, Jennifer, for her love, kindness, humor, and patience in dealing with my life as an entertainer for three decades. I wouldn't have had such a successful commercial or voiceover career without her assistance. Thank you, Jennifer, for always having my back.

I want to extend love and appreciation to my two sons, Evan and Dane. Sons, you motivate me to push even when the odds are against me. My love for you is undying. You are the reasons why I do this.

I thank my brothers, Abraham, Arlen, and Sean. These are three men I can truly trust. Love you guys.

Much love and appreciation to my father, Abraham. Gratefully, as of this writing, he is still with me. I love you, always. #ScorpioSeason.

My mother, Sarah, who passed on Mother's Day, 2015, lives with me daily. Mom, I keep your picture in my wallet. Your life lessons and unconditional love will never be forgotten. I still listen to your voicemails just to hear your voice. Thank you for always telling me I could make it in entertainment when other actors' parents weren't as supportive of their choices. Your love and support got me to where I am today. You will be forever missed, but always in my heart.

My Uncle David Williams passed on Father's Day, June 18, 2018, which was just a couple of weeks before this book was released. Thank you, Uncle David, for being my uncle, brother, and friend. You always made sure I was safe when I came home to visit. I will miss talking with you about football and The Saints! I love you and will never forget you. #myfavoriteuncle

Thank you to my many personal friends, fans, social media friends, and those with whom I've had past relationships. You gave me the fuel to write my first book. I also appreciate all of you who shared your relationship concerns with me online, asking for my advice. You knew that I would "keep it real." This book was motivated and birthed from your life stories.

A special thanks to my editors, Terralyn Shelton Roach and Terri Shelton Rite of TSR Creative. Terralyn, I first met you online, then at a screening for a film I was in. You and your husband have supported me from the gate, and I truly appreciate your editorial input. My first draft was quite raw! Love you guys!

To everyone who ever taught me about screenwriting, as well as authors and novelists who motivated me to write a book, I want to say, "Thank you." Your belief in me helped bring this to fruition.

Most of all, I want to thank YOU who purchased this book. Thank you so much for your love and support. I am sure you'll find its contents to be informative, entertaining, and sometimes very funny, as I've heard every relationship woe imaginable. I did this just for you.

Women aren't the only ones complaining. Many men also have real questions about lasting relationships. Hence, I penned this book to help *anyone* who wants a ring to understand why Mr. or Mrs. Right might be so elusive.

I thank you for your expressed interest and support. May your desire to find lasting love be a dream come true.

-Gary Anthony Sturgis

*"If you focus on results, you will never change.
If you focus on change, you will get results."*

-Jack Dixon

CONTENTS

Preface

Chapter One: Barbie Dolls & Toy Solders............................... 1

Chapter Two: You're Not a Princess; He's Not a Knight in Shining Armor...................................... 9

Chapter Three: Wake Up! You Are the Common Denominator.. 13

Chapter Four: Men Think Like Men, Not Like You!................. 17

Chapter Five: I Repeat: Get Off Your Pedestal!...................... 25

Chapter Six: Make Him Forget the Other Woman................ 31

Chapter Seven: How Competition Works in Real Time............ 39

Chapter Eight: Make Your Actions Match Your Words........... 45

Chapter Nine: Save the Blame Game and Listen!................... 51

Chapter Ten: Men's Needs Are Simple..................................... 59

Chapter Eleven: The Power of the Pussy.. 63

Chapter Twelve: Confidence is Sexy.. 71

Chapter Thirteen: He's Not Your Project; Don't Make Him Over.. 75

Chapter Fourteen:	Miss Independent is Misunderstood............... 83	
Chapter Fifteen:	Your Projection Creates His Perception......... 89	
Chapter Sixteen:	Are You Really "Wife Material?"..................... 93	
Chapter Seventeen:	Your Biological Clock is Your Problem, Not His.. 103	
Chapter Eighteen:	For Better or For Worse..................................109	
Chapter Nineteen:	Get Your Bitter, Single Friends Out of Your Ear.. 113	
Chapter Twenty:	The Ceremony is All About You...................... 117	
Chapter Twenty-One:	After He Takes That Knee............................... 121	
Chapter Twenty-Two:	You've Got Daddy Issues................................ 129	
Chapter Twenty-Three:	He Needs Your Support.................................. 133	
Chapter Twenty-Four:	Master Debating.. 137	
Chapter Twenty-Five:	Trust is a Must.. 143	
Chapter Twenty-Six:	Real Love is Without Condition..................... 149	

Chapter Twenty-Seven:	He Does Not Want to Marry His Mother..	155
Chapter Twenty-Eight:	Sex is Not a Weapon.................................	161
Chapter Twenty-Nine:	Know When to Shut Up............................	167
Chapter Thirty:	Be His Biggest Motivator.........................	173
Chapter Thirty-One:	Accountability is Responsibility.............	183
Chapter Thirty-Two:	If You Don't Have Time, Don't Have a Relationship...................................	187
Chapter Thirty-Three:	Excuses Are Useless.................................	191
Chapter Thirty-Four:	The First Day of the Rest of Your Life...	193

PREFACE

#WhyHeWontMarryYou sheds light on issues that govern a man's choices when it comes to picking a life-long mate. I am not writing this book to bash women or to suggest that men are somehow superior or better equipped for relationships or marriage. Instead, my objective is to satisfy the curiosity of women who are wondering what men *really* think of them as potential wives.

What I offer here is a comprehensive overview of reasons that men won't pop the question. In most cases, the reasons presented are directly related to things women either do or fail to do. It explores what the average man thinks and feels, whether good or bad, while in a relationship. A man usually won't discuss what leads him to either make a permanent commitment to a particular woman, or to push her into the "friend" zone; or to drag out an uncommitted relationship with her into the "no ring" zone. This book shares those secrets.

I've been married for twenty-six years. Having grown up in a male-dominated family with three brothers and no sisters, I can tell women a bit about the mindset of the average man. My mother and father remained married for 54 years until my mother's death. She passed away on May 11, 2015. (My wife was born on May 11th, so this date holds special significance for me.) Given both my parents' example and the fact that I've been married half my life, I feel I can shed some insight on what it takes to obtain, keep, and stay in a long-term, committed relationship. It's apparent to me that women who've had little to no success in this area could use facts that will change the game by putting the ball in their court, that's if they are willing to play.

My insights come from many years of personal experience, observation, and many conversations with a variety of single women from different ethnic, economic, and cultural backgrounds. Over the years, it has become obvious to me that something is missing in the way many women think about lasting relationships. Most who have had several meaningful relationships are totally oblivious to the fact that their own character traits, habits, and behaviors are what put men on "pause" when it comes to choosing them as a wife.

Some assume that marriage is simply about whether a particular man is good or bad for them. But there's more to it. Consider the woman who has gone through several men, none of whom decided to drop to his knee and ask to put a ring on it. Why is that?

Everything in relationships is cause and effect, stimulus and response. Believe it or not, YOU and some of your behavior traits are reasons why men won't commit to you. Sometimes you are directly responsible for things not going the way you desire. There are some behaviors that can even prevent a woman from being able to successfully start a new relationship with the man to whom she is attracted.

#WhyHeWontMarryYou explores a man's perception of female behavior, revealing the very things that bring him closer

to a woman—even to the point of marriage—versus things that push him farther away. The objective of my approach, which will be both direct and, to some degree, unfiltered, is to help women have a clearer understanding of the male thought process. Men are not always open to sharing how they feel or think, so I cover the topic thoroughly here.

There are major differences between males and females, starting from childhood. These differences are often left unaddressed in the many volumes that have already been written about love and relationships. I believe that those differences have a direct impact on how men and women view relationships. This causes a lot of misunderstanding and confusion, particularly for females who long to be married.

Again, understand that this is not about trashing women or big-upping men. It is about helping those who long to be married to see things from a male's perspective. If applied, the insights I offer will increase a woman's chances of making it down the aisle. This information is also very helpful to the woman who is already a wife, but who wants to improve the quality of her relationship with her husband and make her marriage last a lifetime.

As you read these chapters, you will learn about the major differences between two basic types of males. You will also learn what really grabs a man's attention, and what turns him off; what makes relationships last, and what makes them quickly deteriorate.

Of course, to each concept and scenario given, there are

exceptions. In general, however, I point out some of the mistakes women make repeatedly, and why men become gun shy when it comes to tying the knot. There are no absolutes to people, to relationships, or to behaviors, as everyone is as different as their DNA. That's why I often mention *self-assessment*, as in a failed relationship, it's not always one person's fault. Two people participate, so two people are ultimately responsible for its outcome. You will even learn about how some of these concepts affected my own marriage! (#Sipstea.)

Ladies, this book is about and for YOU! It is with great passion and concern that I bring this specifically to YOU. Yes, in most chapters, I will be talking directly to you as if we were face to face; so, it will get a little raw and bumpy at times. But know that my primary goal for #WhyHeWontMarryYou is to open the door for self-assessment, for personal evaluation of where you are now in your love life, where you need to be, and what you need to do in order to attain your goal of becoming a wife.

You will have a better understanding of how men see you, and how this is very distinct from how you see yourself. Trust me, there is a difference, and it makes the difference in his level of commitment. In many cases, you are not projecting what you THINK you are projecting; therefore the "you" that you see is not the "you" that men see, which is one of the main issues this book addresses repeatedly.

Get comfortable, sit back, and let this journey begin.

Chapter One

BARBIE DOLLS
&
TOY SOLDIERS

From birth, little boys and girls are taught two different mindsets that affect their behavior and expectations in relationships once they grow into adulthood. Girls are taught to be maternal while boys are taught to be protectors. Little girls, from the tender age of one, are given baby dolls as their first legitimate toy. Think about that. Babies with baby dolls. You know the kind, the ones that poop, piss, need a bottle? The doll they cuddle one minute, throw on the floor the next; the doll they drag around and sleep with? Yeah, that one. By the time they start crawling, little girls are given this type of toy to play with. By this, they learn nurturing "woman" skills like changing the doll's clothes, combing her hair, even changing her diapers.

The baby girl grows into a young girl who graduates from playing with a baby doll to a more mature, woman-like doll from the Barbie collection. Now, this doll sets the second stage of understanding the female role. Barbie has nicer clothes, a hotter body, a car, and a house! Barbie comes with accessories! She is the young girl's representation of things for which to aspire. However, Barbie's real claim to fame is that she has a male companion named Ken who is the basic All-American, good-looking guy. He also seems to have his wardrobe and life intact. Together, they move into a "dream house" and live out their married lives in this make-believe world.

These dolls not only teach young women life skills, but they also mimic the progression of what is expected in a young woman's eyes. They give the illusion of what happiness and relationships are supposed to look like. So, from a very young age, girls are taught to be nurturing, loving, caring, and eventually, they will find a "Ken" and move into their dream house.

Then there's the story of the damsel in distress; the little princess who is living out her adult fantasy of being rescued from something. Some young girls are instilled with a value system that says this: "You are a princess, and one day, a knight in shining armor will come to your rescue and sweep you off your feet." Man! This is some amazing stuff! If only we understood what we were being taught to believe.

Young boys, however, are NEVER taught these supposed ideals. They are never told that one day they will be required to be a knight in shining armor that needs to save the damsel in distress. A young boy isn't given a doll that has a romantic mate (like Ken). Boys never play in a "dream house," nor are they told that one day, they will need to acquire one. Their young minds are shaped very differently.

While little girls are learning their skills, boys are pulling the wings off insects, catching lizards, fighting, and playing "King of the Hill." They are playing war games with toy soldiers and action figures. They are being taught to be hard, not soft, and how to defend and protect themselves. At no time are these young boys told what young girls are told, and vice versa. Little girls think that little boys are mean and that they stink; they don't yet know that one day, their paths will cross.

Now, make no mistake about it. Many parents tell boys to RESPECT girls and women, but they are not telling boys what they are expected to do once they reach manhood. This is where all issues start; with EXPECTATIONS. Understand that both parties have different expectations.

In time, young men find themselves attracted to young women, clumsily seeking to gain their attention and affections, winging it most of the time. They mess up but learn through trial and error. Because young women were instilled with certain expectations, they don't instantly detect the attraction the awkward young guy feels for them. After all, the young man has just left the wolf pack that consisted exclusively of other young men. And, in those dealings, everything was about aggression. Winning. Being better than, smarter than, and more commonly, stronger than. He is not equipped with the knowledge or skills to win over a young lady. But it's not his fault; it's a fault in parenting. People cannot do what they don't know to do.

But parents have no manuals. A mother delivers her newborn baby, and it's wonderful because the nurses take care of it while she is still in the hospital. Yet, a few days later, she and her mate take the baby home, and just stare at this new little bundle they made together that came with no instructions of what to do from that point on. They just start being parents, which also comes with a lot of trial and error. But that is expected, as this is new to both.

As we become more enlightened, however, we must be careful to pass that information along to our children. We must be deliberate about teaching our young boys what is expected of them when they become grown men, which includes what a woman wants and needs. We must tell them that women expect to be swept off their feet. In all that we do to raise them right, it's one of those things that often slips through the cracks. We need to change that.

When young girls grow up and become young women, they are often disappointed in what appears to be carelessness in men. They don't realize that men simply don't know they are supposed to rescue them and sweep them off their feet. That was only taught to the girls, not to the boys. These dream-like stories become real-time nightmares as men approach women with caveman-like mating skills because they simply don't know any better. Most of their time was spent beating up their friends, playing sports, and just being boys. So, because boys were never given the same narrative that girls were given, young women become disappointed and disillusioned. They realize this Barbie fantasy is sometimes just that—a fantasy, and not a realistic expectation. Now, this is no slight to those men who figure it out, as many do. But we all know it doesn't come on their first try. They learn through trial and error.

We must also accept the fact that times have changed dramatically, and the older traditional gender roles have shifted. Gone are the days when men worked to provide for the household all by themselves; the cost of living has also affected the love game. Jobs may downsize or may pay too little to maintain an acquired lifestyle. Due to this and several other factors, women have become a powerful presence in the workforce that men depend on to help with the family's financial needs. Women are now required to be more than just wives and mothers; they are also co-providers of finances for the household.

Because the woman has also become a breadwinner, she has learned that this comes with power and some say-so. Like a man, she now feels she can afford to have more verbal input as she, too, is paying for their lifestyle. And she is correct. I personally think relationships work better when both parties share in providing for the household and making business decisions. Men should be more open to accepting the shifted roles of women and the changes in relationships that have resulted. Financially, she is now doing what men have always been expected to do. Therefore, it seems only right that she is regarded as a 50/50 partner.

Many women I chat with share the belief that a man should

treat her like she is the only woman on earth. But here is why this is a ridiculous expectation; she is NOT the only woman on earth. Assuming what she has to offer is far greater than what the woman standing next to her has to offer is a dangerous way of thinking. That other woman might be more open and capable of securing that man if she is willing to do what it takes to get and keep his attention.

Does this mean that the other woman is better? No. It simply means that the other woman is better for HIM. Women must lose this notion that they are the end-all-be-all for any man. They are the end-all-be-all only for the man whose attention they can get and keep, not every man that steps up to court them.

Keep in mind that a woman is taught that one day she will be a wife to a hero, not man. A man doesn't know to be her hero at the outset. His objective is to just get in her pants. This is how he feels he is special to her as she allows him a closeness that she won't allow just anyone. A woman, at this same early juncture, wants to be heavily courted. Her mindset is *"show me how much money you can spend on me in the hopes that I will let you sniff it."*

Men and women are different. What he wants and needs is not the same as what she wants and needs. The sad part, when it comes to sex, is that it's supposed to be a fair exchange. But for a man to get it, he must first make all time, money, and events all about her. So, the question in the back of his mind becomes *"what exactly is she doing unselfishly for me? If the sex is a mutual endeavor, what is all this wining and dining for?"* Men waste tons of money trying to impress women who can very easily decide at some point they should stay in the "friend zone." This makes men very hesitant to invest in them, as they can spend their money on anything instead of using it to impress someone who doesn't understand their needs. It's one-sided, and in time, the man who never gets to the part of the relationship he wants to enjoy will become bitter and turned off.

Now, I am not at all saying men shouldn't court women. But women also need to keep it real about what men need while enjoying the courtship. She needs to understand that relationships involve two people, not just one. Both must be willing to give and receive to keep it fair, happy, and long-lasting.

"So, why is this book directed to us?", you ladies may be asking. Ladies, it has been my observation that a good number of you have a distorted view about the roles men are supposed to play in relationships with you. This is to open your eyes to what you may not have known while waiting on that proposal. The objective, as stated earlier, is to help you see yourself from *his* perspective, as he was raised with a different set of values. Gaining insight into the mind of a man will help you to know the changes you need to make in your core beliefs about the role you play in your interaction with him.

Chapter Two

YOU'RE NOT A PRINCESS; HE'S NOT A KNIGHT IN SHINING ARMOR

Here is a fun fact: A woman can size a man up pretty fast. She knows within the first five minutes of meeting a man if she will go to bed with him. But the man doesn't realize that once he starts talking, he will lose "pussy points." This means he is totally unaware that what he says and how he behaves can rapidly diminish his chances of getting her in the bed, though he thinks he is spitting top-flight game.

Most of you ladies know whether a man is your type or not, but you get caught up in the spending, buying, and gifts while forgetting he is doing it for a reason: to eventually have sexual relations with you. If you already know that will never happen, why accept his gifts? All you are doing is setting yourself up for future arguments, as this man will eventually feel that you are only using him. He's not your knight in shining armor. He's human and has feelings just like you. You women can be just as carnal as men, but it's simply not fashionable for you to be sexual, as it comes off as "whorish." Openly admitting to your sexual drive knocks you off that pedestal you wish to live on when marriage material rolls up. So, if you wish to be perceived as virtuous, you shouldn't sleep with every man who takes you shopping, nor accept a lot of free gifts from men with whom you don't see a real future.

You want a husband, right? Therefore, it is imperative to understand that decisions you make while you are young will affect your options later. Your bad choices will limit the quantity and quality of good men who would otherwise be interested in you as a lifelong partner. Babies by random men, bitterness from bad past relationship, etc., will impede your chance of finding permanent love. If you carry this baggage from one relationship to the next, you will make each new man suffer for things someone else did. It's self-sabotage.

More importantly, young women also need to have more realistic expectations in what they seek in a long-term mate, and, find out what they need to bring to the table to acquire such a man. The princess who wishes to become the queen needs to be able to accurately identify the prince who wishes to be a king. This comes from having a clearer understanding of the mindset of men, as well as developing a realistic assessment of yourself.

Ladies, not all issues you will encounter with men will solely be their fault. The woman who reaches her marriage objectives will be the one who can not only identify issues in her man's character, but also identify issues in her own character. Self-assessment is equally as important as pointing fingers and assigning blame to your mate or potential mate, as you may be the cause of some of the challenges you have in your relationship. It takes both parties seeing themselves in true light and making necessary adjustments.

Relationships only end up "happily ever after" when the work has been put in. Fairytales are just that, and don't represent what real-life relationships are made of. You can only be responsible for your part. Seeing things from a man's point of view helps in understanding why men make the moves they make, and why he may not feel you are the right one to be his "forever."

This information is important not just for those of you who wish to be wives. It's also for you ladies who have gotten the ring but are having a tough time maintaining the relationship after his "I do".

Chapter Three

WAKE UP! YOU ARE THE COMMON DEMOMINATOR

In my talks with many of you ladies, I hear lots of bitterness because of the way men have treated you. I see it all over social media. Many of you are frustrated with how men move. But, the funny part is that you complain about men that you let into your lives. Yet, you take no responsibility for it. If you're saying on social media that you hate men because you were mistreated by a couple of dudes, then it's time for SELF-ASSESSMENT.

Too often, I observe that women spend too much time blaming men for all their problems in relationships. They rarely take any responsibility for their own behavior and happiness. Ladies, it's not a man's job to make you happy. Happiness is something that comes from within. If it's not already there, I promise you, he will not be able to bring it to you. It's far too much of a burden to put your need for happiness on another human being, as he is responsible for his own happiness, too.

Don't think of a mate as a "better half," as a man is as whole as a woman, and vice versa. No one completes another unless one was born a half person. People can only enhance each other or subtract from each other. We should all seek out mates that complement us and enhance us, not complete us as if we are less than whole.

A man and woman should be companions for each other, not parents, owners, or bosses. Ladies, very often, while you think you are demanding equality, what he really hears you saying is, *"I am better than you and above you, and I am to be worshiped by you as if I am the only female to ever set foot on earth."* You are not his "better" anything, so lose that train of thought. Even the Bible states that man was lonely, so God created woman from his rib. Think about that. Man was lonely. The role of woman was to be a man's companion, not his boss, his role model, or a deity to be worshipped. So, save all that business for church.

Often, in conversations about relationships, I gather that many of you ladies seem to think that you are the super wonderful jackpot for that man. But, if this were true, wouldn't you be engaged or married by now? Again, this is the time to self-assess. Let's say you've dated five men and these men didn't know each other. If you had the same issues with each one of them, this can only mean that the common denominator was YOU. What is it about you that attracts these types of men? You are the only constant in all these bad relationships. When you get this "I am the shit" mentality out of your mind, you will find the answers. Like him, you are flawed. We all are. No one is perfect in any relationship, so both parties must make allowances for the other's flaws in order to peacefully coexist.

Most women LOVE to tell a man their issues with him in great detail. Yet, they become quite defensive the minute he has a real problem with something she does. I've experienced that many times myself. Denial itself is a huge flaw. Yes, men do it all the time, but, so do women. Accepting personal character flaws is something none of us enjoys, especially when the criticism comes from someone we care about.

Women often look at men as projects. Ladies, men are not something you can fix or make into what you want him to be. Just like you can't turn a whore into a housewife, you can't turn an asshole into a husband. Just like some women aren't marriage material, neither are many men. If you are seeking a husband, you need to know the qualities in a man you desire and stop believing you can get Tyrone Rough Neck to transform into your ideal mate. He showed you who he was, but you keep trying to raise a grown-ass man. You can't do it, so stop trying.

When you choose a mate who you know won't make a great husband, don't be mad when he fails you, as you knew better when you started seeing him. Not every man is meant to be your husband. You need to use this simple rule of thumb when dating: Choose a date that would make a good mate. Don't hop on every fine lap you run across. Some people are just for fun and experiences, not for life partners, and you shouldn't have any expectations of longevity from these types of men. You won't marry every man you give "some" to, so don't expect them to see a wife in you because you slept with them. If you have had a string of bad relationships, at some point you need to look in the mirror and say, "Some of this is on me." Many women never do. It is far easier to paint a perfect picture of self and blame all those who didn't appreciate it. If you keep attracting the wrong types of men, take ownership and explore your own motives. Do you see these men as projects that you need to correct? Are you in tune with all his faults but completely blind to your own shortcomings?

When you drag bitterness from one relationship into the next, causing the next guy to run for the hills, it will make you feel that men just can't come correct. No, it's not that they can't come correct. They just see damaged goods, and that's simply not attractive to them. No man wants to waste his time hearing about the mistakes the last guy made, and he definitely doesn't want to pay for them. To push the envelope even further, no one wants a wife with a nasty, bitter attitude. To you, this may be coy and sexy; to him this is a headache. Realize that.

I will remind you repeatedly to REMEMBER THE OBJECTIVE. The objective is to be the wife of a great man; and to do so, you should get a better understanding of what that means in real-time for both you and that awesome man you want to desire your hand.

Chapter Four

MEN THINK LIKE MEN, NOT LIKE YOU!

From girlhood, most women dream of having the perfect wedding. They think of the colors they'll choose, how many bridesmaids they'll have, which of their friends will participate, and where it will take place. Guys, by contrast, have no such visions or plans. Even if the relationship advances to marriage, they don't participate much in the planning of the wedding. This goes back to those different mindsets taught from birth. Young men just don't know what women expect until they are told.

Guys are generally clueless about the grand marriage plans. And they tend to figure it out once they start liking the scent of a particular woman. It usually only comes up with most men when she expresses the need to go to the next level after sex. For him, the next level after sex is simply a second try at sex. It seems that for a woman, however, there is an invisible vein that goes from her vagina to her heart. She must realize there is no invisible vein that goes from a man's penis to his heart. At the outset, sex to women is far deeper emotionally; but to him, it's *"Finally, I hit it. Damn! About time!"*

Ladies, you need to give the man time to feel what you feel. Don't force on him all the emotional commitment you envision. Even after he makes it through your 90-day period of celibacy, he will not just automatically fall in love with you because you figure it's time to give him some before he becomes bored and completely loses interest. You have to give the man time to see your VALUE. Sex is not the value; it's just what he desires. No matter how well you sucked it or rode it, he still doesn't see you as a wife. Yet, in your mind, the sex sent you to heaven and now he is your "Mr. Right." This doesn't necessarily make you his "Mrs. Right." Just trying to keep it real with you.

A woman must allow time for a man to feel any special way about her, and with most men, it won't happen overnight. Many women feel an emotional bond shortly after their first sexual encounter, as most only give of themselves when they feel a meaningful connection to the man. To keep it real, some women are just as forward and carnal as he is, and she just wants to screw, knowing full well that he is not the type of man that she could ever truly fall for. In the typical scenario, however, she tends to get to an emotional space much sooner and wants to force him there before he is ready.

Sex may spark feelings in a man for the moment, but it won't keep him there. After the sexual act, he is back to his senses, but now, open to learning more about you. Although he now feels a bit closer to you physically, he has not yet arrived at the emotional place where you want him to be. Give him time before you scare the crap out of him by moving too fast. Just as you may feel he is moving too fast sexually, he may feel you are moving too fast emotionally. You may not know when or where you are showing this behavior, but he sees the red flags clearly.

A man will begin to withdraw when you start using phrases like *"So where is this going?"* too soon in the relationship. He will experience these conversations as your effort to force him to move at your emotional pace. You need to let him get to where you are on his own, and in his own space and time, just as you did when deciding when to give in sexually. Just as you need to feel comfortable going at your own sexual pace, he needs to feel comfortable going at his own emotional pace.

A man doesn't become emotionally attached from sex alone. It bears repeating: You must learn patience. In the meantime, show him other reasons why you should be his only choice. For him, sex is never the sole deciding factor when choosing a wife. If it were, every man on earth would be married. But many aren't. Sex alone is easy to get anywhere without attachment.

When a woman is stuck on her pedestal, she is fooled into expecting a man to chase her. Instead, she should be showing him reasons that he should choose her to be his wife. This is where a woman has far more power and control than she realizes. She needs to be more proactive in what she shows versus what she says. Any married woman will tell you the reason her husband popped the question is that she never stopped showing him why no other woman was better for him.

She wasn't fooled into thinking that the sex alone was enough to hook him. She made him see her VALUE. And, she saw his value and made sure he knew it.

A complacent woman who waits for a man to "get it" will find herself, not only waiting, but in time, competing with other women who are giving him what he wants, perhaps with greater ease and less complaining. Ladies, you need to remember that whatever you won't do, another woman will. A man is attracted to those who cater to his needs. He's the one who has to ask YOU to marry him; so how are you winning by making him see you as a difficult choice? If you want a husband, step off your pedestal and show him you are the one for him. Men love that.

A man can see when a woman is willing to invest in him, his career, his life, his wants, needs, and desires. The woman he will marry is the one that builds him up when he is down, steps up when no one else will, and comforts him in his struggles. Men want to feel important to their mates, but so many women are living in a ME, ME, ME space. Such self-centeredness in a woman can eventually turn a good man bad and push him to start seeking to fill his needs elsewhere. "Elsewhere" means the women you all call bitches, THOTS (that hoe over there) or whores. Actually, these are the types of women who, unlike some of you, see the value in a man and are willing to pursue him to get him. THAT is the kind of woman he will consider marrying, as he knows she will always be there for him and have his back.

Ladies, if you are too selfish to support your man's goals and dreams, I promise you, he will lose interest. You must honor his core values and life aspirations, as these were in place before he met you. If something has to go, you will be the odd woman out. When you start to slip in your support for him while harping on your own needs, he will stop fighting you over his needs and get them met elsewhere. So, don't be salty and call that woman out of her name. To her, all you are is the woman in the way of her real happiness. Your issue is not with her, but in your relationship with your man. If your relationship matters, now is the time to find and fix the issue so that you can continue to build and grow together.

Engage in self-assessment by asking this question: "Why is my man cheating on me?" Don't waste time getting mad at the other woman as if she owes you some blind loyalty for sharing a monthly cycle. She is not your problem; YOU are. He is turning away from YOU. Let go of the blame game, the name-calling, and the self-pity. Instead, carefully consider what you may have done or not done to run your man to another woman. Clearly, the other woman is filling a void you created. Ask yourself, *"What am I no longer doing that once held my man's interest?"* My advice to you is to not only start doing those things again, but innovate them, reinvent them, keep them new and fresh for him. In this way, you will regain his attention. If your objective is to get him to see you as a potential wife, remember that "wife" says "lifetime." You can't just show inconsistent flashes of interest and brilliance. A man won't wife inconsistency.

It's always easier to blame someone else for things you neglect to do. I strongly believe it will be beneficial to be a bit more proactive in assessing your own choices and behaviors and consider how they may affect the man with whom you desire a meaningful and lasting relationship. Sometimes, he is just reacting to you. Rather than argue with you (some women view arguing as "attention"), he will withdraw and seek whatever the relationship is lacking in someone else.

Is it right for him to venture outside of the relationship? No. Sometimes, however, it's how a man deals with issues you present. A man may be unable to express how that little irritating thing you often do really makes him feel. So, he first becomes defensive, then combative, then he shuts down on the subject altogether. This is where he becomes open to gratification elsewhere.

Ladies, here's the truth: Men really *do* want to marry you. They just don't wish to do it on your terms or time. You must be patient. Please understand that men don't care about your biological clock, monthly period, mood swings, or desired timelines for marriage. They will make a move with you when they feel they are ready to forsake all others, not when your clock says so. You can't pressure a man to do things you want until he is on the same page. They can feel when you are desperate for them to move at your pace.

Don't give him an ultimatum. I promise you, that this will sever his feelings about any plans of a long-term contracted arrangement with you. Demanding pre-wife treatment and putting out prerequisites shows him you are not a good long-term choice because you are already making everything about you. In all you do, remember your goal is to show him the reasons he should wife you.

Ladies, if all your relationships start out great, but eventually fizzle, chances are it's because you made it more about YOU than about "US." The men noticed it in your words and behaviors. They concluded that, long-term, the relationship would end up being more of a headache than a coup. There is no "I" in team, and a selfish woman, no matter how beautiful, will end up alone. Single women have the option of having everything their way without having to consider anyone else. That's a selfish woman's better option.

Chapter Five

I REPEAT: GET OFF YOUR PEDESTAL!

You say you want a husband. But you also want to be a trophy in a trophy case. That, to a man, makes you just an item in a window display, not someone who is attainable. When you see a man you desire, step down off your pedestal and show him your willingness to walk with him, not in front of, or on top of him, but alongside him. He is not going to spend his life looking up in awe at you. This expectation is what I like to call the "Pedestal Mentality." There's nothing wrong with wanting to be admired. To become a potential wife, however, you need to be catchable at some point.

Men long to hunt, as it is in our nature. For us, the magic is "the chase." Even once you're caught, you must be mindful that men are still hunters. Locking him into something long-term doesn't erase his innate hunting tendency. So, instead of being the woman who acts like she is the Queen of England, be the woman he can't stop thinking about, the woman he longs to chase and catch again and again. This is far more attractive to a man and gives him the feeling that you are someone who will be around for the long run, not just a temporary fix. You totally have the power and ability to keep his full and undivided attention, even if you neglect to use that power.

The reason most of you women don't apply this power is because you live in too much of your own reality and not the man's. I have encountered many women who don't understand that when you put yourself on a pedestal as if you are a prize, a man will quickly tire of trying to be impressive, as it becomes a one-sided endeavor. He will then seek a woman who will make his chase worth the effort, and you will lose the man you thought was your future.

Instead of waiting for a man to automatically notice you, do what it takes to make yourself noticeable. He will notice you if he sees in you a partner and a support. And, always be consistent, as the minute he likes it and you take it away, his interest in you will fade, as this is what HE really likes in YOU. You can't become lazy and complacent just because you got his attention. Getting someone's attention is easy. The mission now is keeping it; falling back into your aloof, princess ways will never accomplish this goal.

Sure, your pedestal may be cute at first. But once you know he is the one you want, HE needs to know it. Many women make the mistake of showing this interest with "marriage" conversations and "where is this relationship going?" pressure. This is moving too fast and he won't respond favorably. However, if you can avoid making it all about you, he will see you as distinct from other women, and will pay more attention to what you are offering. A man wants a mate who shows equal interest in his life, his goals, and his dreams. He wants a wife who is supportive, not discouraging. Be this woman, and he will step up to be the man who wants a wife, not a girlfriend.

Keep in mind that YOU want a husband; but for now, he wants some sex. He does not walk into a relationship seeing a wife. You have to be the one to paint that picture without pressuring him with timelines or rushed commitment. When you do it right, he simply drops to a knee and pops the question. But, it will never happen if you spend your time thinking you are "the shit" and he is "the smell". Men who see that kind of selfishness will bail. He needs to know his worth and value to you, and it cannot come in the form of demands and ultimatums. And, from a man's point of view, ultimatums say, *"When I marry this woman, every time I don't give her exactly what she wants when she wants it, she will threaten to leave me."* Just like women, men want to be secure in knowing their time is not being wasted.

Ladies, courting you is an ongoing expense. While you're constantly expecting free gifts, you need to realize he has expectations for all this spending, wining and dining. Do your part and meet the man halfway. And let me be clear: NOT YOUR VERSION of halfway. Your version is sometimes wrapped in your own terms. Instead, meet him halfway by giving attention to what he likes, wants, and desires, even if his preferences are different than yours. This will show him that you are willing to invest your time and energy into what matters to him, not just what matters to you. This is only fair, since you are not losing any coinage in the courting phase, and you are both putting in equal time.

Show the man you desire that you know when to step off your pedestal. Unless you want to be the proverbial side-chick, or the stereotypical "baby momma", you might want to come down off that pedestal and be in the moment with him. Aloofness is only sexy to you. Trust me.

Unrealistic Expectations

I want to see you win in the game of marriage, but I do believe some of today's women have seriously unrealistic views and expectations of a husband. I hear many younger women talk about material things like cars, big houses and "red bottom" shoes, as if the man's primary role is to be a Santa Claus or a walking ATM. At no point do they mention what they can offer in return. Driven by arrogance and selfishness, they want as much material gain from the relationship as they can get.

Many women come with a built-in "I am the shit" attitude, and "ANY man would be lucky to have me." If this is you, what are you offering that is so lucky for any man to have? Just being "you" is only impressive to YOU, but it does very little for HIM. Single women with this mentality have the wrong idea of what to expect from a husband. You see the selfishness all over social media. Many of today's women are doing such a great job at loving themselves that a man wouldn't feel his love is necessary.

On one of my many social media posts about relationships,

a married friend of mine, Terralyn Shelton Roach, posted this comment: "Even when I talk to some singles, some of their ideas about having a husband disturb me." Terralyn then quotes some of the women she overhears in salons, one of which said, "If he can't get me what I want," and, "If he doesn't want to do things my way…" Terralyn notes: "They aren't looking for a husband, they want a butler who can't talk! This is no match for partnership in building a life together. It is wonderful hearing a man express his thoughts. I sure do love hearing mine express his."

Terralyn's observation is extremely valid, as she has been married for more than three decades and knows a thing or three about keeping a marriage together.

Get rid of the pedestal mentality. Men are not machines to be ordered around. They don't just exist to provide for your material wants. Men will not marry self-centered women, no matter how pretty or fine they are. Those who get lucky won't maintain a marriage for long, and if so, not a very happy one. Marriage is not about control; it is about partnership and compromise. Those unable to partner or compromise will not have a long and fulfilling marriage.

The pedestal mentality wins no awards. Allow your man to feel important. Men want women who are willing to walk with them and develop the relationship through love, compromise, and mutual respect.

Chapter Six

MAKE HIM FORGET THE OTHER WOMAN

L adies, realize that you are not the only woman alive. Know that other women are attracted to the same man you're eye-balling. They are also on a mission to have him. However, many of you women may feel uncomfortable competing in the dating department. This is especially the case if you have the "I am the best thing God ever created" attitude. Believe me—you're not. You are just one of MILLONS of great things God created, and, guess what? The other "great things" want the same thing you want: A husband. So, here's the question: How do you get him to see you and only you?

First, you have to accept the fact that other women are turning his head. Instead of being mad about it, revel in it. Who wants a man that no one else wants? Clearly, if a man is attractive to you, he's also attractive to many others. You may not want to compete for a man's attention, but it's the twenty-first century. How we approach relationships has to progress with the times.

You cannot keep living in the 1960s. We are now in the

new millennium. Gone are the primitive days of riding a horse or walking to the next town to be with a woman. Technology hasn't made it any easier for women of virtue, as cell phones and iPads enable people to participate in the "now" generation, when everything is immediate. Today, people send pussy and dick pictures via text. So, while you're playing hard-to-get, someone else has already sent the thong pic, the breast pic, the clit pic, and the ass pic. I know you don't want to hear it, but men like that; it's sexual. Men are visual and sexual by nature. So, he will always be more attracted to the woman who is showing him he can get it and she wants him to have it. Old-school women need to find a gentle balance between playing hard-to-get and showing him what he could have.

I'm going to keep it real with you ladies, because these are the facts. A nice rack will turn his head any given Sunday. So, beat her to the punch and show him what he could be getting. Do this, however, only if you feel he is the one. You have to keep it spicy, even when you can't see him. You must keep his focus on you. Again, what you won't do, someone else will. Don't be mad when they do, and he is drawn to it. Men will be men, and they are pretty simple. If you listen, they will tell you what they want and expect from you. Too often, women like to be heard but don't like to listen. Men also want to be heard. We will address this point more fully later.

My own experience is a good example of how men view sex and the "other" woman. I personally never wanted to be married. It was the furthest thing from my mind. Being career-oriented, I never envisioned having the time to meet someone with whom I'd want to go the distance. But I met a girl named Jennifer in college, a nice girl with a big butt and a pretty smile. (The song "Poison" by New Edition hadn't been written yet, but I digress.)

Jennifer is still my wife to this day because she did what no other woman did in college. She stuck around because she saw my potential, not my popularity. At the time we met, I was winning Greek step shows as a member of the Theta Mu Chapter of Omega Psi Phi Fraternity, Incorporated. Consequently, I was quite popular.

As a young college student, I was doing well in my acting career; so, in my mind, my life was on track. Jennifer saw my potential and promise. She also saw the plethora of women trying to sleep with me, and at twenty years old, I liked a lot of them. My Daddy told me as a child (and, in front of my mother, I might add): "Son, fuck them all, bar none." I followed his advice to the letter. I was a young Alpha male who had been popular most of my life in my city, and when it came to young women, I had my pick.

One day, I was putting our Greek show trophies in the University Center display case and glanced at Jennifer. I knew immediately that she was someone I wanted to meet. Little did I know I had caught her eye, and she felt the same way about me. Despite my popularity, I was corny as hell when it came to women I actually liked—you know, the women that weren't slanging it at me. So, when I saw her again a couple of weeks later in the University Center, I stopped to speak with her, not knowing when our paths would cross again.

To gain some points, I introduced myself to her using my frat name, which was "Batman." Given my popularity, I was known as "Batman" everywhere in Louisiana, from the University of New Orleans to USL in Lafayette, Louisiana. Usually, whenever I introduced myself to the ladies in this way, I got a very favorable response. Not quite the way it played out with Jennifer. This woman had no idea who I was, so her response was simply, "Your momma named you that?" I swear I was not only embarrassed, but I knew right then she was someone I was willing to put my time into, as she had no preconceived notions about me.

Jennifer was not only unaware, she had no interest in my popularity. I found that to be attractive as hell, and we exchanged numbers and began dating. It was nice to have met someone who was not into me because I was popular, so I was able to build a foundation based on real attraction. It would be some time before she came to understand just how popular her future husband was.

A few months into our relationship, I was ready to hit it. She came to my dorm room, we made out a little, but when it was time to go all the way, she was on that "90-day" rule. I got all aroused and ready for action for nothing. *Forget that*! I came up with some lame excuse about hanging out with my frat brothers to abruptly end our little make-out session. As soon as she hit the door, however, I grabbed the rotary phone and began dialing a girl I was dating low-key in the dorm. (Millennials: Google *rotary phone*.)

Karlyese had helped me when I pledged, and I'd known her for a while. We had an amazing sex life, so she was my first call. However, a few minutes later, my roommate and suite mates came in warning me that Karlyese had come up the elevator and Jennifer saw her headed to meet me. I didn't realize that Jennifer was still at my door hearing me make the call on the loud, old-school rotary phone. Karlyese knew I was dating Jennifer and was courteous enough to remain in the next room as she waited to see how this would play out. I got a knock on the door and opened it to see a dejected Jennifer.

"So, you couldn't wait, huh?" she asked.

"No," I responded. "You get me rock-hard daily and give me nothing. I got needs. Now, I respect that you're not ready, but I am. So, you can wait as long as you like; just don't expect me to." I had to keep it real with her.

On this night, she realized *if I am going to keep this man, it's time to put out*. So, we finally slept together, and I finally started taking her seriously. Now, I became really interested in getting to know the soul of who this woman was, and she began showing me she had my back on a regular basis. It was no longer one-sided. She understood that my needs were real. More than just giving in sexually to my needs, she made sure I ate, got me around to auditions, and helped with our Greek shows. She made herself a part of my life and growth. She was truly wife material, and her actions proved it.

What my wife did that other women usually don't do is she played by the rules of the show, *Survivor*. The rules are outwit, outplay, and outlast. My other sexual partners would meet her and tell me "You won't ever leave her." One by one, they each went on their way. Unlike the other women, Jennifer SHOWED me she was the one who would be the last woman standing. She dealt with the wild child I was, living young and free in my popularity. Instead of saying "Forget this," she saw her future husband, and simply kept showing me I didn't need all these other women as they would not be around when school was over. She would.

Ladies, THIS is why I married her 6 years later. She SHOWED me she should be my WIFE and life-partner. Meanwhile, other women were disappointed because I didn't choose them after a few rolls in the sheets. Although they took care of my sexual needs, they weren't invested in my goals, in my shows, or in anything past hanging out and just having sex. Jennifer, by contrast, saw my potential as an artist, got me to move to California, then positioned herself as a receptionist in a Top 10 commercial talent agency, keeping my photo face up on her desk until the agents asked who I was.

Jennifer assisted me in building my career and my dreams. With her support, I was eventually able to make enough money to enable her to leave that job so that she could stay home with our young son.

Ladies, THIS is how you get a man to marry you. Stop making it about you. SHOW him your value, don't expect him to simply see it. Remember, he is a man and is hunting, so become his most-desired prey. Know when to give in; don't keep running as he will stop chasing you, and will go, instead, for an easier target. As of this writing, Jennifer has been my wife for 26 years. That's pretty good for a man who never saw himself ever married, which is a huge testament to her undying and unconditional love.

Don't seek immediate validation. Instead, learn to compete. There are many other women after the same man you want, which gives him options. If you think he is the one, don't be afraid to get in the game and vie for his attention. Now, if you are resistant to the idea of competing for his attention, this may very well be the reason why you are home alone reading this book (no shade intended.) You're in a good place, however, because you are open to learning a different approach. Your willingness to learn and change could mean a whole new beginning for you.

By your actions, show your man that no one else matters more to you than him. Isn't that what you expect when you want validation? Don't you want to feel like the center of the universe to him? That comes with a mutual exchange. By competing with others for his attention, you are validating him in the same way that you require him to validate you. Don't be lazy, expecting him to automatically see your greatness, because he won't unless you show him.

Even while married, you must still compete. Women who see that you have a keeper are not shy about wanting what is yours. The life you created on paper is for a lifetime, and when you become lazy and complacent in the course of your marriage, your husband may seek the attention he is missing elsewhere.

Chapter Seven

HOW COMPETITION WORKS IN REAL TIME

My own two affairs are examples of exactly how this plays out. Yes, I said affairs. See, you probably thought this was going to be a "bash the women" book, when my true objective is to speak openly and honestly about how we men view things. We are far from perfect, so I will use some of my own choices to illustrate the points I'm trying to make.

Twice in my 26 years of marriage, I have fallen in love with other women, and have had full and meaningful relationships that almost lead to divorce. To preserve their anonymity, let's call these women "Angel" and "Bella," two names that will come up from time to time from here on.

They were both beautiful, model types. One was brown-skinned, tall, smart, sexy, resourceful, and extremely talented. The other was light-skinned, slim, sexy, resourceful, and extremely focused on work. Both were Cancers with many similar personality traits. Angel had two kids from two previous marriages, while Bella was single with no kids and had never married. Both were classy ladies in public, rarely drank, could hang a dress and walk a runway in heels. In addition to their looks, their talents were equally attractive. Talent is sexy to me.

Neither relationship started out personal or intimate. Angel and Bella were each people that I worked with closely, and these relationships were never supposed to happen. Understand that with men, what catches the eye may be your beauty, but what keeps their attention is your heart and spirit. These women both inadvertently found a way into my heart, but both were also the type that don't share or play second well. For this reason, at some point, an ultimatum was inevitable.

At various times in my marriage, when things were not the way I wished them to be, I allowed myself to see in other women what I wanted in my wife. I was attracted to women who were still allowing themselves to be hunted. I was a hunter growing old and tired, and as life was driving a wedge between me and my wife, others were beginning to hold my interest.

Both Bella and Angel had several traits I saw in my mother while growing up. They were both very much into their appearance. Just like my mother, they always kept up their hair, clothing and personal image. That was familiar to me, and thus, very appealing. My mother shaped the way I viewed women; therefore, I always noticed the ones who maintained themselves.

I became close to Bella at a time when Jennifer decided to pursue some of her own goals. She left work in the entertainment industry and went back to college to fulfill her dream of being an interior designer. I had become Jennifer's support system just as she had been mine until my career took off. But I started to feel alone and began to wonder, "Who's going to help me build now?"

I was attracted to the idea that Bella and I could build an empire, as that is what Jennifer and I had always done, and it kept us together. This possibility is what drew me to Bella. It became clear, however, that she was willing to help everyone BUT me. In time, this behavior would tear down our relationship and destroy our friendship for life.

Initially, the "other" woman seemed to fulfill a need that wasn't being met in my marriage. Over time, however, I came to realize that something was seriously lacking in each of the outside relationships. Bella was the type that was all about herself and everything had to be her way. She wanted everything to happen according to her timing, yet, she was piss-poor at time management. When she wanted something, it was, "Stop what you're doing; I want it now!" But when the situation was reversed and I needed her attention, it was, "Wait! Help me do this first." Eventually, this would lead to debates and fights. People make time for what really matters to them.

Many women want the title of "wife" without the responsibilities that go with it. "Wife" sounds better than girlfriend, or side-chick, or jump-off, or the other labels that society assigns to women who fall in love with married men. Since I had been in a committed relationship for so long, however, I knew what I needed in a long-term mate. And, I knew what I could and couldn't deal with.

Angel had been married before and had kids, so she had a better understanding and a bit more patience than Bella. Bella was on the biological clock, but Angel was different. Angel was also an artist and producer who knew how to be a wife, as she had done it before. I might have seen a future with Angel, but she had health challenges and I was unprepared to meet her long-term needs. She always helped me make money, produced a lot of great things for me, and was a long time real friend that backed her words with actions. She is one of the exceptions to the rule when it comes to being a wife. She would eventually marry again, showing that even a woman who has been married twice with two kids can still make a great wife to a deserving man. I was happy to see her find love again and remarry.

To salvage my marriage, Angel and I had to stop communicating altogether, and we did. I still speak to her eldest son from time to time, but we have not spoken in almost a decade. We each made the choice to take responsibility for our own lives.

Blame is only appropriate when you or your mate have eliminated self from the equation of the issue. But, as in most relationships, you are both to blame for some portion of the problems you face. You need to work it out if you truly matter to each other. This is the only way to survive the obstacles that will affect your marriage as you persist in developing and growing your relationship.

Ultimately, neither Bella nor Angel could compete with the nurturing ways of my wife. Jennifer always knew when to make it about me, about our family, about friends, and about us. She even knew when it was necessary for her to make it about her. My wife made it hard for me to walk away, as no matter how awesome other women were, they didn't have the "wife" gene Jennifer has. Jennifer is relentless in her love and devotion, something that has been apparent, not just in her words, but in her actions all these years. Having known this kind of love since college, it would take more than a fine body and some fun times to make me walk away.

Chapter Eight

MAKE YOUR ACTIONS MATCH YOUR WORDS

Ladies, regardless of what you say, it won't take a man long to realize when there's no room for him in your life. Bella never had time for anything but work, and often worked way past her scheduled hours, as she got her validation from opportunity, not people. She didn't value our relationship, but was always saying, "I want to marry you and spend the rest of my life with you, build a business with you and have a kid with you." Yet, this woman made no time to build anything from assisting me in my efforts in business to being available for my needs in a personal way.

Bella wasn't suitable for the wife role. She lacked honesty. Her words said she wanted commitment, but her actions showed she was always one fight away from saying "it's over." This is not what a man seeks in a wife. Why would she expect a man to walk away from two decades of a marriage on a whim, knowing that tomorrow, she could change her mind? A man can't be expected to take this kind of foolishness seriously. Actions speak louder than words.

Learn to give your man what he requests without always making him wait or reversing things to make your desires a part of the deal. After all, when you want something, you don't want to wait; you want it now. So, why should he have to wait until later? At times, genuine love requires putting your man's needs ahead of your own. Don't always expect a payoff for being generous. He needs to be reassured that his success is important to you if you expect him to get on a knee at some point and propose.

Women fall short with men when they set dynamic relationship goals that they put forth little or no effort to reach. Time is the one thing you will never get back. It is a huge commodity, so no one with a brain wants to waste a lot of it. This is called the OVERSELL. Many women oversell promises that appear to fulfill even their own dreams; yet, they don't put forth the time or effort to make such things happen. This leaves the man wondering how he bought into her words while time proved her actions didn't match. Pretty soon, she will read as "full of crap" to him, a liar, and a fake who just says what feels good, not what's really in her heart.

This is the type of woman expecting the man to sweep her off her feet, when her feet are never present to be swept.

How was I supposed to see a wife in a woman who simply wanted the title, but not the job? She can't cook, hires a maid to clean, is not attentive, makes time for neither me nor "us," and at my lowest points, bailed when I needed emotional support. A wife needs to have her priorities straight starting with being a real friend to her husband and keeping the marriage first. If she couldn't make time during the dating phase, it wasn't going to happen in a marriage.

Bella was the type who made no time for the relationship. I was married with two teens and had more time to devote to the relationship than she had. She wanted to be a wife but had no wife-like qualities. She was a pretty, classy, stylish, and well put together woman. But everything with her was *"I do this for me, I wear this for me, I rock this for me."* Her "ME" behavior left nothing for me to do. A man wants to feel he is needed in some way. Women who do it all themselves for themselves usually die by themselves.

Don't get me wrong, independent women are very sexy. But when a man comes to believe there is nothing he can do for her because she does everything for herself, he will go elsewhere. Men want to feel needed. Being wanted is awesome but being needed is what really motivates him.

You can't give a man mixed signals and not expect him to see it. When your words stop matching your actions, your relationship is in danger, adding more wasted years to your journey. When you say something to a man, he expects it to happen. When you disregard your own words, he starts to doubt your validity and sincerity, and eventually, he'll start to pull away.

You can tell your man something as simple as, "I'm going to send you a sexy picture as soon as I get off work, Baby." But, when you get off work, if he doesn't get that picture, or even a call, he will be taken aback. If you then hit him up the next day from work with "Hey Sexy!" as if he forgot the picture you promised the day before, he may call you out on it. Own your mess-up; don't defend your broken promise. At that point, he doesn't want to hear anything but a sincere apology, as you disregarded him.

Ladies, you can't talk all that good sexy talk to your man while at work and then fail to follow through. Don't get him all hot and leave him hanging, especially when you are free later that day and have the time to make those fantasies come true. Don't expect him to still believe you and get all excited all over again about what you have in store for the next night. You don't keep your word, and word is bond. Those little things mean nothing to you, but trust me, he is judging how he feels about you and how close he will get to you based on how well you keep your word. A man won't marry a woman who is a tease, whose words are meaningless, and who makes promises she doesn't keep.

When you need a bill to be paid, you want it now. Treat your man's wants and needs with the same immediacy. You will be a much happier woman because he will make sure of that. The woman who is attentive to her man understands that this is a dance and that both parties must be mutually accommodating. Women who get this will find themselves wed. A really good wife knows when to both step backward and forward. There is a time for both to either lead or follow. Like a choreographed dance, we waltz together in harmony and it all works. But the minute I am waltzing, and you are twerking, we're headed for trouble.

I have met and talked to many women who need excessive attention, praise, and validation. It's quite annoying to me and would be to the average man. We will give a woman praise and validation when she does what is praiseworthy, not just because she requires it on a daily basis. The minute a situation is not totally about these women, they get upset. If you need constant validation and praise, I suggest you date yourself. You will be happier because only you know how needy you are.

Believe it or not, even if he never says it, your man appreciates it when you show him you are selfless and that you know this journey is for the long haul. If you are patient enough to build the relationship, you will see in the future that there will be many days that are all about you. But for now, let it be about him. In this way, he will see that you care about his feelings, that you have his back, and that you are true wife material.

Chapter Nine

SAVE THE BLAME GAME AND LISTEN!

Men could easily stay single forever and have as many fun, casual, uncommitted relationships as they want. Marriage is YOUR objective, not necessarily his. He needs time to learn that marriage really is his objective too. You, however, must be the one to change his mind. STICK TO YOUR GOAL. Placing blame elsewhere for past failed relationships will only derail you from your goal of becoming a wife.

You see it all over social media. I get into debates on this topic all the time. When women fail in relationships, they sometimes tend to cast all men in a negative light, when it's only the last dude they were sleeping with who was the problem. A good example of this was a memorable post on my Facebook page where a woman declared, "I will never date another black man." Her statement implied that all black men were to blame for her unhappiness.

This, of course, started a viral spiral of responses from slightly offended black men who felt compelled to chime in. The woman couldn't understand why dudes were going in on her so hard. So, I joined the conversation to explain why she was getting such negative feedback. Like many women, she asked men to explain their motives, but didn't LISTEN to their responses. It was almost like a rhetorical question, as she really didn't want their answers. Seeking clarity, the question she posted after her initial post was, "Why are so many brothers mad about my post?"

Ladies, when you post a question to men on social media, try letting them respond without converting their opinions into a debate. When you become combative, men realize you don't value their opinion, as you are too stuck on your own. I was thinking, *Damn woman! You clearly are getting a lot of blowback from the post; accept the answers to your question!* A lot of women simply can't do this because they have already processed it in "woman think." Ladies, men don't think like you. To understand what HE is thinking, let go of how YOU processed it and listen to his response. You can't understand his point of view if you can't get your own out of your head.

Here's a rule of thumb: If you think it, but he is saying it, focus on his version. Seems many women just want to hear what they want to hear, not what they need to know. The woman on Facebook was incapable of understanding how blaming all black men for one man's failure was unfair. I get it; she was upset with her guy, but she had no reason to assume that guy's behavior is the behavior of all men of his race. It is hilarious to me that women even do this.

This woman started a whole new debate about her right to

date whoever she likes. No one challenged her right to date freely, but it was unnecessary for her to down all black men just to assert her right to date non-black men. She refused to see why the men perceived her comment as unduly harsh. She was intent on asserting her opinion and felt that the black men on her timeline should have no say about it. When women generalize blame in this way, they are not seen as ready for marriage. Like it or not, it's just not sexy to us.

So, the woman who posted the comment is now upset that black men are defending black men. Women like her don't understand that when you blame all black men for the flaws of a few, you are downing your own entire race. She was defensive with practically every man who responded, all the while asking, "What is wrong with my statement?" What was wrong with her statement was that she attributed the behavior of the one who hurt her to all men of color. Clearly, this would read offensively. What's even funnier is she kept asking these men why they felt the way they did about her comment. As they tried to answer with long paragraphs to explain, she didn't accept what they had to say.

This is another issue that makes men pause. When they realize you don't care about their responses, they will simply stop giving them. Men find it frustrating when you ask them questions, only to ignore or dismiss their answers. You tend to live with the answers that are in your own feelings and heads instead of accepting the ones you requested from them. When men see this, they will end up being less honest with you.

They figure you can't handle the truth. Rather than argue with you, they will simply shut down all their emotions and not engage with you at all. They begin to perceive you as a bitter, hurt soul, and their input is not helping you, but rather, is frustrating them.

Since no one on that Facebook post had any vested interest in this woman's opinion of black men, we all simply stopped engaging with her. She lost out on possibly gaining the right kind of attention from any of the men who might have been inclined to talk to her. Her stubbornness may have cost her a meaningful relationship. She was unwilling to listen.

Some of you women tend to blame men for all your woes. You chose the man, let him into your life, home, and body, but then you blame him for just being himself. In fact, you might be wondering who this man really was to begin with. The truth is, however, that all of us--men and women, alike--have at least two selves: The *ideal* self and the *real* self. And, they usually look nothing alike.

The ideal self is almost like a representative we send out into the world to show the most likeable, agreeable, successful and acceptable aspects of who we are. The "representative" is the best part of everyone's personality, the in-tune person who shows the time, care, and concern needed to progress further in the relationship. Each one of us has a "representative" that we dispatch to make sure we are as impressive as possible. But when the "rep" is gone, the ideal selves disappear, and the real selves begin to emerge. You both begin to see each other's crazy sides. The relationship starts its slow and painful downward spiral. And this is where the blame game starts. Blaming the man prevents you from accepting responsibility for the part you play in the relationship. The same is true of a man who blames women for his failures, but never takes a hard look at himself.

The woman who wrote the angry Facebook post showed her pain, but her disappointment was misdirected to all black men, versus the man or men who actually hurt her. Even if her anger was warranted, she will never move forward until she reflects on where she stood in the problem, on how long she allowed it to continue, and how she plans to avoid unhealthy relationships in the future.

I speak with many women who have allowed the blame game to become deeply rooted in their feelings and emotions. "He did this to me, he did that to me," they say. So, here's my question to them: "Why did you tolerate all that?" The response is usually the same: "Because I love him."

All relationships have friction, but when the friction develops into pain, you have to step back and figure out what you may be doing to cause some of the disdain you are getting from him. Many men are not in tune with their feelings, so they will not always openly say where their anger is coming from. You have to find a way to get your mate into a place of open dialogue. It will NEVER happen if you are constantly pointing a finger of blame at him.

If your man is suddenly acting differently toward you, trust me, you've very likely done or said something to cause that change. He just isn't as open with his feelings as you are, nor does he want to argue with you. So, instead of verbalizing what the real issue is, he just shows you with a change of attitude. This is also a common tactic for women who struggle with communication. It is rarely effective, however, and later causes many harsh words to be spoken. This only worsens things.

Sometimes, it is necessary to take a step back, breathe, and reconsider the approach. With patience, you can learn how to read your man's attitude shift and get to the heart of the matter.

I can't say this enough: STICK TO YOUR OBJECTIVE! Don't get caught up in negative feelings. Both parties are sensitive when problems arise, but if you want this man to marry you, try to understand things from his perspective. A woman who is full of petty emotional debates while just dating will highly annoy him in a marriage. Instead of coming at him in your emotions, try to calm down first and then speak with him, engaging him in a rational conversation without casting stones.

A man doesn't respond well to constantly being accused or blamed for things, but he is capable of hearing and listening when you approach him in a respectful manner. So, just talk to him. Your desire is to be heard, and he doesn't hear you when you are emotional, yelling, or being disrespectful. It only opens the door for him to do the same to you. In most cases, men surpass women in their ability to be cold and brutal; so, don't argue with him. Don't put him on the defensive. Once this line is crossed, no one is sticking to the point. Instead, tension only escalates, and the real issue remains unresolved.

Arguments that veer off track in this way can quickly become dumping grounds for even the smallest of unspoken irritations that were left to fester for a long time. Don't hold things in until they are boiling hot, as you won't get to the resolve that you are seeking. What you will get, instead, is a serious fight, which sets your future marriage back each time. Stick to your objective.

Learn to master conflict resolution and you will be a happier woman. Why? A man who loves you and isn't pushed back by emotional outbreaks is willing to show you just how true his love is. Remember, you are seeking a husband. How effectively you communicate with him will determine how fast he takes a knee. He needs to be comfortable with you. No man wants a nagging, complaining woman who is always on the verge of an emotional explosion. Learn to curb the emotions and use calm words instead.

In our marriage, we rarely play the blame game. Sure, there are times when an accusation is warranted; but we each know how to tell the truth and take responsibility. In my two outside relationships, however, the "blaming" dynamic was very different, and there was plenty of blame and guilt to go around. In each case, I was open and honest about being married from day one. In both cases, these women made a conscious choice to proceed in a personal relationship with me, regardless. Both Bella and Angel allowed love to make them want to be wives rather than just girlfriends. But neither of them would do the things necessary for me to see them as wives. Still, they each demanded it.

Chapter Ten

MEN'S NEEDS ARE SIMPLE

Compared to what women require, a man's list of needs is fairly short: Keep him sexually and mentally stimulated. Cook something. Stay out of the room on game day unless you are a fan of the sport. Don't start nagging the second he gets home. Let him get in and relax a minute from his trying day. He is not your girlfriend and doesn't like or want the daily gossip; save that for the ladies.

By contrast, the list of things it takes to make the average woman happy looks like a scroll to men. For every 5 things you need, he needs only one, but he can't get that one without doing 20 of yours. I am telling you now, ladies, this is how your relationships begin to unravel. You are just as responsible for meeting his needs as he is for meeting yours, but he is always thinking your list is severely long. When you can't do the simple things on his list, he starts to purposely neglect yours.

If you want him to respect you, be respectful. If you want him totally into you, you need to be totally into him and show concern for his wants and needs sometimes. Men quickly tire of women who complicate what is simple and who prove to be difficult. Very often, this behavior is a desperate grab for attention.

The tendency to complicate can be perceived as a "take-over" attitude, something men never appreciate. I see this when I post various topics on social media. Some women will read the post, but instead of responding to the topic, they reverse it against me, or make it an attention-grabber for themselves. The need to take over in this way is a major turn-off for a man.

Here's a specific example: On my Facebook page, I do a "Freaky Friday" post, asking my female friends, fans, and followers what color panties they're wearing for the day. The post is popular and is always written in a humorous, lighthearted tone. Overwhelmingly, my fan base finds this fun and entertaining, and always responds accordingly. Yet, every week, there is someone who responds whose intent is to complicate what is meant as simple fun.

My Freaky Friday post attracted one woman who always refuses to respond to its context. Instead, she either reverses the question by asking me what color I was wearing, or she calls me a pervert, or she tries to change the subject altogether. If the post offends her, she could easily just bypass it. But she never does. She feels compelled to comment, yet refuses to stay within the boundaries of what is posted and play along like everyone else.

As other women happily participate, this woman insists on being the opposition. In her effort to steal the spotlight, she even goes as far as trying to change the topic. She attempts to take the position of power by posing questions she expects me to answer while disregarding the conversation I initiated. She could easily initiate topics on her own Facebook page; but instead, she'd rather play "dictator" on mine.

This woman needs to allow those of us who find humor in my Freaky Friday debauchery to enjoy the moment instead of trying to change the whole dynamic to make it about her. Any man on my page who sees this kind of behavior can't help but to think, "*Here is a difficult woman.*"

Women set themselves up for failure when they go about getting attention the wrong way. This woman clearly wants my attention but goes about it in a way that neither I nor any man would appreciate. If her objective is to attract a man on my page in hopes of him seeing her as a potential partner, she is failing miserably. Her discomfort with the topic is not my problem. It's her problem and she needs to just leave it alone instead of being a nuisance.

It is commonplace for some women to be self-centered and controlling, but to a man, it's extremely annoying. A woman who won't stick to subjects at hand, who tries to take over what he is doing, and uses her selfishness to rob from what gives him joy can count on staying single. No man wants to make a commitment to a woman who is more interested in being combative than supportive. It just won't work for him.

Women like the one on my Facebook page show traits that cause men to flee. Exit stage left! Men see them as a long-term headache; so, no need to hit it short-term. Women like this love to put themselves in a position of debate, which throws off the entire focus from the subject presented to them. Everyone on that Freaky Friday post can see the debate, and it is distracting. This type of woman will be nothing more than a side-chick, or an occasional hit and run, but nothing ever serious.

Chapter Eleven

THE POWER OF THE PUSSY

The vagina. You got it. Men want it. But how you use it will determine if a man will want to marry you, or just hit it and quit it. Just like you women, men love sex. If the lovemaking is good, he will want to stick around. However, if you are the type of woman who has a difficult personality, even good sex won't be enough to keep a man. In addition to great lovemaking, a man is seeking a real companion for a lifelong journey. A potential wife must bring other things like loyalty, trust, attentiveness, and time. Much of it starts, however, with amazing sex.

Consider what marriage is to a man. He is basically taking himself off the market for other available women, as you are taking yourself off the market for other available suitors as well. For a man, this means no more variety, so what you are bringing better be awesome. You are asking him to have the same meal for the rest of his life. The right woman can do just that and make him forget everyone else. Make yourself that woman. A man who wants a wife is seeking a lady in the streets and a freak in the bedroom.

Even a woman who brings kids into the relationship can use the power of the pussy to lock a husband. Sex is a main priority and need of a man, so if you keep him happy in this department, there is a stronger chance you can get him to marry you. If the sex is bad, the relationship won't survive. This alone should tell you how important it is, as there are consequences for both parties. Sexual chemistry keeps a man coming back for more, allowing you to take the time to get to know each other on other levels. Good sex makes him want to explore your mind, get to know your history, and perhaps, build a future with you.

Go back into your sexual history if you have one. It is very rare that ANY woman gets sprung off of a condom dick. Something about raw sex offers a real connection that women cannot deny. The ones that you get sprung by sexually are not wearing condoms. Intimacy can happen with a condom, but the connection is very different without.

Review your history of sexual partners and ask yourself how many wearing a condom stole your heart and time. I am willing to bet the ones that moved you the most emotionally were the ones with whom you had skin-on-skin raw sex. Funny when you think about it. The level of intimacy is closer, the trust is closer, and the emotions become very real.

Your sex life has a lot to do with this man's decision to marry you, to stay married to you, and to refrain from sleeping with other women. Sexual intimacy is the cornerstone of the relationship. When the sex is great, you keep that man's attention; when it is not, it not only causes chaos, but that man will start to seek with someone else that intimate bond he once had with you.

Turn on that sex appeal, as it will draw the man closer to you. Once you have him close, you can begin to show him why he should stay there. He will get to know the depth of your personality and soul, your likes, wants, needs and desires. You will also be able to tell if he is the right one for you long-term.

The simple fact is that you women hold all the cards when it comes to sex and interpersonal relationships. How you play those cards will determine many things, such as how many options you will have in the mating pool versus just the dating pool. My wife's parents told her, "Pick a date that would make a good mate." This is valuable advice for young women.

You know at the outset that some guys you meet would be nothing more than a fun time. So, choose who you share your vagina with carefully. A man who wants to marry you would like to think you don't have a hundred "bodies" on you, with multiple sexual partners falling out of the wood works. Sure, he has had quite a few, but bear in mind that none of those women became his wife in the process either. So, what makes you any different? How you use the pussy is what makes you different. You have to use it in a way that makes the man never want to leave you. Remember--don't use it as a weapon.

Learn your man and what he likes, realizing that what you won't do, another woman will. There is no shortage of women who will be more than willing to do whatever to take your place. Don't open that door.

But, Don't Brag on the Vajayjay

If you managed to find a marrying type of man, you have to know you aren't the only one who sees his potential. But never worry about what other women are doing; just focus on what you are doing. He sees you both, but the one that gets the ring is the one that shows him she will be there until the end. He is not seeking the one who thinks her stuff doesn't stink, or, that her vajayjay is the best on earth.

Let me break it down for you. There is nothing special our unique about your vagina. MANY women told me while single and married that if I slept with them, I would be sprung. Really, Boo? Really? Or, my personal favorite, "You have never had pussy like this before." No, let me correct you: I have had TONS of pussy like that before, just not that one. Unless it is cut horizontally or is detachable, I have had it before. Just because a few happy men said it was amazing doesn't make it amazing for everyone. Men will say any wet hole is the bomb; so, all this bragging on your vagina needs to stop. It's makes you look ridiculous.

Okay, I need to go there. Have YOU ever had sex with YOU? You just walk around with a vagina and maintain it. If a kid can pass through it at 10 pounds, I don't care how big a man is, he isn't big as that! So, all this *"my shit is so tight"* is an exaggeration you are using to make men want you, for the wrong reasons at that! I have met a few women who are quite tight in that area, but not many. But still, why talk about your vagina to men if you want them to think of you as wife material? Every woman has a vagina!

Many of you know I can pitch a baseball from across the room and you can catch and swallow it between your legs hands free. Part of the reason is because you've let too many men in, thinking it would impress them. Ladies, you act as if none of the women prior to you ever rocked the man's world. Just like a penis, you still have to know how to USE it. And just like men who brag on their dick and stroke game fall short, so do women who brag on the pussy. My experience suggests that women who brag in this way are usually the laziest in bed. So, stop broadcasting about your vajajay! You are more than that, or, at least you should be.

The Double Standard

If you are into a hot guy, other women are too. So, like it or not, you have competition. But, he is probably noticing you, too. In fact, you may have lots of male attention, but here is the difference. Your virtue won't allow you to explore many of these options. The more you share of yourself with men sexually, the less attractive you are to the ones seeking a wife.

Although it is an increasingly unrealistic expectation in the twenty-first century, men still wish to marry virgins, or women who have had a limited number of lovers. Sorry ladies, this is just how society works. He can bed 100 women and be considered a stud, but if you bed 100 men you are considered a whore. No man wants a woman on his arm that other men can talk and laugh about while sharing their history of meaningless experiences they had with her. So yes, there is a double standard.

On a funny note, both men and women lie about the number of lovers they've bedded. The general math on this is that men tend to round up 20, while women tend to round down 10. For example, if a young man is asked how many women he has slept with, if he's only slept with 2, he will say 20 – 22 to appear more virile. However, when a young lady is asked the same question, she may have actually slept with 12 men, but will say only 2. Just as men want to impress with their conquests by rounding up, women want to downplay their experiences so as not to be considered a slut. So, we all lie about our sexual background to be impressive to the opposite sex. Men don't want to be seen as virgins, and women don't want to be seen as whores.

Women love sex just as much as men do, but most like to suppress this fact to keep the appearance of class. It's alright ladies, we like you a little freaky. Just don't be like that with everybody, okay?

A man can sometimes have some freaky requests, but, if that's not for you, that is not the man for you, plain and simple. I'm not suggesting that you should compromise your personal preferences or convictions for any man. Wait for the one who has the same interests where sex is concerned.

A man isn't going to stop liking what he likes just because you won't perform it. You have to simply cut your losses and move on to someone who is more your speed. This is fair to him and will save you later heartbreak when he starts cheating.

Men will tell you what they like and desire, so either become open to his level of freakiness, or let him go. Only you know your limitations. You must be true to yourself and real about what will and won't work for you because you have to live with you even if no one else does. You will meet someone more your speed; no two men are exactly the same.

Never Mistake Sex for Love

Ladies, you need to be careful of the "L" word. You tend to be quick to say the words, "I love you" just because you had an orgasm. If you want a man to be your husband, let him say it first. When a man says, "I love you" first, his actions will soon follow. When you say it first, you are putting pressure on him to reply with the same, when he may not quite yet be on that page.

Remember, men don't fall in love from good sex alone. That's a myth that many women believe. The man that wants to marry you will mention the "L" word first because he means it from his heart and will do everything in his power to prove it to you. Watch for his actions long after the sex is over, or he just may be saying, "I love you," because he is feeling good after his orgasm. If he says it without the sex and shows it by being more attentive to your desires and needs, he means it. This is the man with whom you can have a real future.

Love is a beautiful thing, but adding pressure to it can destroy it.

Chapter Twelve

CONFIDENCE IS SEXY

A woman who knows her intrinsic value and exudes confidence is very attractive. The biggest barrier to confidence for most women, however, is their size. I know women who are well over 200 pounds with very high self-esteem. Consequently, rather than being depressed about their weight, they carry themselves like they know they are beautiful. And many of these same women have HUSBANDS, while some smaller, supermodel types wonder why they are alone. Size only matters to some men. However, confidence, a good heart, selflessness, and attentiveness go a long way with most men, regardless of what your shape or size might be. Even if you are not as attractive as a cover model, your level of confidence can be very intriguing. To a large degree, a man will regard you in the same way that you regard yourself. There is someone for everyone, so become confident in who you are and what you have to offer.

Don't dump your insecurities on your man, as it will surely turn him off. Even if he stays around, he will quickly tire of your constant need for approval and validation. Do not put him through such nonsense. Know your value; know your worth. If you lack confidence, it's an internal issue you need to work out yourself.

Confront your inner issues and resolve them. Don't put the weight of your insecurities on your man. That's your responsibility as he has his own issues to deal with. A man's role is not to boost your self-esteem. How can he affect how you feel about YOU? He can't. That's why it's called SELF-esteem.

Confidence goes a long way; we're all drawn to it. I have found that even larger women who don't fit the conventional commercial definition of "fine" by American standards are highly attractive and desirable when they exude extreme confidence. But when a woman displays self-consciousness, a shamed face, or talks down on herself, men will avoid her.

The problem with insecurities is that they bleed into your relationship, which makes a man feel he must constantly stroke your bruised ego. Over time, his compliments and constant encouragement will seem like a waste of time because you reject his affirmation while consistently demanding more of it.

I've noticed that after the ring is acquired, many women think they can slack off. The sexy lingerie is replaced with flannel, the random sex is replaced with child rearing and bills tend to challenge their comfort level. So, they challenge their husbands' sexual needs as well. No one wins when the game of "tit for tat" begins. In the case of my wife, like most wives, she once became too comfortable and laxed. The weight came on and less time was put into building my career. She was also sharing too much of our pillow talk with a single friend who never presented herself as a friend of our union. Women push for a pinnacle, a zenith, the "next level." But what level comes after marriage? Divorce.

The woman who desires to be a wife needs to take these things into consideration, and practice acting like a wife in advance.

Ladies, you cannot become complacent once you get the man to sign on. If you kept your hair maintained before marriage, continue to do so throughout the marriage. If he was into your size, try to maintain it as much as possible. You want him to keep that income flowing in steadily, right? Would you be okay with him being complacent, playing Xbox or PlayStation all day when his job downsizes instead of tenaciously seeking another one so he can take care of you? I think you get my point.

Chapter Thirteen

HE'S NOT YOUR PROJECT; DON'T MAKE HIM OVER

I hear many women say they want a "good" man; a God-fearing, one-woman man, that consummate gentleman with a great job, nice car, and six-pack abdomen. They say they want that guy that opens car doors, sends flowers, and comes straight home after work on time every day. This is the dream man most women describe when speaking about what they want in a mate. Some women THINK they want this man, until they get him, and quickly find him boring. Why is this? Because they really want the bad boy type. Let me explain more about these two types of males: The *alpha male* and the *beta male*.

The Alpha Male

The alpha male is the most desired of all males, and he is usually quite untamable. He is the guy men want to be and women want to be with. The untamed, rough-around-the-edges type is what seems to really attract the ladies. This is the man who not only has it going on but knows it and just doesn't give a damn about what others think of him. He is the man that keeps women emotionally on edge. This is the man most women find very attractive, but it's not the man they SAY they want to marry.

Many of you ladies won't admit it, but some of you are driven by the alpha male because he makes you feel something, even if that something is "stressed out." You are drawn to men who keep you on your toes, be it positively or negatively. If this is you, admit it, at least to yourself. The men that gave you the most challenges in relationships are the ones that stole your hearts, minds, and vaginas; nevertheless, you remain attracted to that fire and energy.

Ladies, you can say all day that you want a "good" man, but you often find him, and then, find him unattractive. "Why is that?" you should ask yourself. But you don't, and won't, because you just like what you like.

I have observed that women seem to be drawn to situations that keep their emotions engaged, whether that stimulation is good or bad. Men who in some ways drive you insane in both the bedroom and in daily life are challenging. Whether male or female, we all love a good challenge.

I talk to women all the time who speak on the supposed "good men." They are always saying how boring these men are even though they are kind, considerate, generous, gainfully employed, and they make time for them. But deep down inside, there are many women who enjoy a good challenge.

Even some of the bad-boy, alpha-male, career-focused types

eventually make for good long-term mates; they are just harder to pin down. These men are always attractive to women across the globe. Tons of bad-boy alpha types are very successful in their business lives, so I'm not trying to paint the picture that all bad boys are of the criminal variety. They do, however, have a huge audience of available females that will court them because women love this type of man.

The alpha male doesn't easily yield to a woman but is the one that usually draws her attention. Though most desired by all women, he is the hardest to lock into a marriage. There is great competition for his affections as this man has many options. He doesn't fall in love too fast. If you want him as your husband, you have to be willing to compete for his time and attention.

The Beta Male

The beta male is much different from the alpha male. The beta male is the type of man that will keep you on that pedestal you love. He is the type that will send flowers, massage your feet, and even take your yelling and screaming at him because he is in awe of you. This is the man that will never leave or cheat, so the power of the pussy works extremely well on this type of man. He is the man that loves you more than you could ever love him, so your heart is safer with this type. He will never break your heart, as the possibility is that you will break his first. This man will kiss your feet and jump off a mountain without a parachute for you. He is a dream and what most women SAY they want. There is only one issue with this type. Over time, this man may become too predictable to you, which is odd because he is usually doing everything you said you wanted and needed from a man.

Many women tend to walk over these nice guys, even though they claim this is what they are seeking. Seems to me, what they are really seeking is a bad boy they can MOLD into this nice guy, as they don't want a bad boy in his entirety either. Women often step on the "good" man, bypassing him for the headache that comes with the bad-boy type while saying they want a good man. "Good guys finish last" is not just a common expression; it is often reality.

What is wrong with a normal, responsible man as a life choice for you? Only you know the answer, as you meet and bypass them all the time, or immediately slide them into the "friend zone" because they cannot hold your interest.

Now ladies, what makes you think you can turn the "bad boy" into a husband? Many women think men are projects that they can tailor-make into their perfect ideal. Men are not clay that can be molded into your dream. You have to accept them as they are. When a man shows you who he is, believe him.

Here is the reality: The average man will chase you down, the alpha male will not. The average man is where you developed that false sense of security and over confidence. The alpha male breaks all that down in a heartbeat. He will keep you upset as you see your average attempts to get his attention don't resonate with him like they do with the beta male. From time to time, you may grow frustrated because he is not easy to tame, but this is to be expected. Your skills in the area of seduction will position you to keep his attention, but your character, potential parenting skills, and support of his goals will keep him. If only women really wanted the beta male, aka, the "good guy," they would actually be better off. It takes persistence, time, and effort to get the alpha male. But, it is possible.

I can't repeat this enough. This is the hardest part for many women to accept; but the truth is that, in order to keep the alpha type, you have to step down from your pedestal and engage with him. He will not chase you like the beta male. He will not immediately fawn over you like an average man who is in awe of your femininity. You just being yourself won't be enough to lock down the alpha male; so, YES, you have to put in some work. You can easily get his attention, but you can't keep it without effort. He is attainable, but you will have to use the power of persuasion, which starts with mastering the power of the pussy.

You want the hot, sexy man with ambition, or if he's already accomplished, with wealth and success. He is the one you will work the hardest to lock down, because you are not and will not ever be the only woman holding his attention. Don't be afraid to go the extra mile when you see the alpha male you want, because he is open to having that end-all-be-all woman. You just have to step up and show this man you are what he needs.

Women need to be more honest with themselves about what they want in a mate. If you say you want a very dependable, predictable man, but are always gravitating toward the "bad boy," you are contradicting yourself. If you are drawn to men that keep you on your toes, accept that this is a mental challenge that usually leads to mental stress. Don't try to transform an alpha type into a beta type, all the while expecting him to maintain the "edge" that attracted you in the first place.

Ladies, if you truly want a good man, stop bypassing him when he appears. No, he won't be as exciting as the bad boy, but he will provide you with the ease and stability that most women claim they seek. However, there is a surefire way to know what you really want. Just check your dating history. That will be your biggest proof.

If your past is full of stormy, rocky, and intense relationships rather than, pleasant, stable, and predictable ones, chances are you are not seeking a good man. You are seeking a man that provides excitement and stimulation. Ladies, there is nothing wrong with this, until you start trying to change him into what he is not. You can't tame and domesticate a wild beast, no matter how hard you try. This causes the emotional rollercoaster rides you experience with such a man. But, no matter how many times you say you are done, you never really are.

Women need to be real about what they find attractive. Want, need, and desire are not always the same. Sometimes, the person we say we want is not always the best fit, the one we really need. We all have to accept there is no perfect man or woman. We have to choose mates and learn to tolerate their shortcomings and revel in their strengths. What you cannot do is change a person or force them to be who you want them to be. If you really wanted the nice guy, or the good guy, he wouldn't be just on the "friend" list in your life; he would be in your bedroom.

So, if you really want the good guy, why didn't you date him? I'm sure you've had several to approach you. What you may really want is the challenge of turning a bad boy into a good man. But again, men are not projects to be worked on.

Ladies, not every man you date is husband material. Some relationships are just meant to be experiences that make you better for your marriage, in the event a man you love ever chooses to ask for your hand. By all means, be more honest with yourself about exactly what you are seeking. At the very least, accept the man you choose for who he presents himself to be, whether good or bad, until he shows you otherwise.

Here is a general rule of thumb: The person with the least amount of interest in the relationship controls it. Put another way, when engaging with the so-called "good guy" type, you will get the level of loyalty, fawning, and devotion that you dream of. If you truly prefer the bad boy, however, the good guy's loyalty and devotion, however intense, won't be enough to retain your interest. The good guy is always at your mercy, and at any moment, you can walk away.

If you choose to tough it out and get an alpha male, love and embrace him with acceptance and understanding. Your love for this bad boy can also turn him into a meaningful marriage partner down the line. Bad boys want love as well; they just have more options so they are harder to reel in. However, nothing is impossible if he sees in you the wife of his dreams.

Chapter Fourteen

MISS INDEPENDENT IS MISUNDERSTOOD

Most twenty-first-century women pride themselves on being independent, both mentally and financially. However, some complain that men can't handle their success or hustle. But that's not what men can't handle. In most cases, it's their independent ATTITUDE that presents a problem.

Many women with the independent mindset think quite like men. They have laser focus, and nothing will come between them and their coin. Believe it or not, men are attracted to these types of women, but they usually aren't the alpha male.

A man likes to see a woman go out and do it for herself. What he doesn't like is when she allows her busy work schedule to interfere with the time and attention he needs from her. People will always make time for what matters most to them. A man shouldn't feel that he is repeatedly on hold because of his woman's career goals. Sometimes, an extra hour on the self-made hustle can wait if it means having quality time with someone who is supposedly important. Life will surely pass this woman up if she can't make allowances for other things beside work. There must always be a balance.

Sometimes, you independent women have extremely high standards when seeking a mate. There is nothing wrong with standards, but be realistic. Some men you meet may not be as far along on their career paths as you are. Don't overlook them just because your success arrived first. Remember when you struggled to get your business off the ground? Acknowledge that same drive in the man you want to marry. You want a man who supports your grind? Be supportive of his.

Many independent women (the alpha female) carry the alpha male gene and treat their relationships with the same low regard as many men do. This doesn't bode well for the independent woman who seeks a husband. In a relationship, a man is seeking a nurturer and companion, not a business rival. The attitude that many career-driven women have keeps a lot of good men at bay. She may see her hyper-focused attitude as a strength, but he sees it as arrogance. He will always applaud her success, but her future as a wife will be in peril if she doesn't consider it a priority to invest in a relationship.

A strong man respects a hard-working woman, but still expects his relaxed and in-the-moment mate when they spend time together. During their private moments, if all her thoughts are still consumed with work, he will still feel like a second. That relationship will surely die. Both parties are responsible for the quality and the quantity of time necessary for developing their bond into a possible engagement and future marriage.

I hear many independent women say, "I have lots of men who asked me to marry them," yet they chose none of them. Now, a man would have to feel some kind of incredible way about you to ask for your hand; but NONE of them qualified? How did they ever get close enough to see you as a potential wife if you don't see any of them as someone you'd ever consider marrying? Who deceived who here?

You independent ladies who pass on so many potential suitors are the ones with the standards that are perhaps a bit too extreme. Somehow, the men you meet are never good enough. This is also another variation of the "pedestal" mentality, where seemingly every man falls short. But, my question to you is this: "Are you really that perfect?" We all have flaws, and the goal is to find a mate who can see our value even with our imperfections, and vice versa.

I am sure most of these men didn't quite qualify, but at least ONE should have. After all, you dated them all long enough for them to have husband-like feelings toward you, so someone wasn't keeping it 100. It was probably you. I'm sorry, but it's just not adding up.

There is often a big difference between what you THINK you are projecting and what men actually perceive. If the confidence you feel you exude is perceived as arrogance, it will be a complete turn-off. He looks at you as a potentially difficult woman. Though he might love a challenge, he won't compete with your attitude and delusion which you hold close. The relationship will fizzle, but you will walk the earth continuing to say, "He simply wasn't ready for all my independence."

I've heard many women say their current man wants to be married because "that's all he talks about." Well, if that's the case, why aren't they married? Some women love the IDEA of marriage, but not the real-life commitment. They relish in the notion that many men supposedly wanted them as a wife, or, their current man wants them to be his wife, but they just aren't yet ready. They enjoy the chase as much as men do, but don't really want to "settle down," even though this is a major conversation with their single and married female friends.

The same woman who won't give a "Yes" to any of her "potential husbands" will tell another man, "If you don't want to marry me, let me go so I can find someone who will." If what she's saying is true, then she simply enjoys the IDEA of being married but has no real desire to take the plunge. She just likes being desired. Lots of independent women fit this mold. No one is good enough, but they don't wish to be alone, so they date long-term, just as many men do. They are alpha females. And, they often grow old to be well-off, lonely females.

Make no mistake about it: Men love you strong, independent women. But, they can do without the bitchy attitude that some of you like to incorporate into your self-made success. No matter what you do for a living, or how much coin you rake in, a man who chooses you as a wife will expect moments of "wife" from you. You can't display blind loyalty to your business, career, or current employer, and expect a husband to understand. A smart, independent, and wise woman understands the true value of maintaining her role as the focus of his life. And the smart alpha female knows when to step up and step back in her role as a mate, and never lets her station rule her household.

Both parties are responsible when it comes to making quality time to build the relationship into something that resembles an engagement. It won't work with just one person putting in all the effort. Being independent does not mean being inattentive. Learn how to balance your career and what you have with your man, and you'll be an incredible wife.

Do your thing, independent ladies, but lose the attitude. It's so not sexy. And be more open to the men who approach you. Don't miss out on the love you deserve.

Chapter Fifteen

YOUR PROJECTION CREATES HIS PERCEPTION

WIFE is more than just a title or a female birthright. It's not a prize you win on an award show. It's the highest honored position in a man's personal life. And, what you PROJECT creates a man's PERCEPTION of you. That's what determines if you are worthy of his eternal devotion. It's not what you think about you, but what HE thinks about you that matters, since HE has to be the one to choose you.

You may see yourself as a prize catch; but, do men? Make sure the wifely characteristics you THINK you embody are actually translating clearly to him. Do some self-assessment to face the reality of what you are projecting to others. If you find that no one is asking for your hand in marriage, perhaps the way you perceive yourself is a bit different from how others perceive you. Maybe the man is not easily buying into what you're projecting. Your projection may not be what you think.

Some of you aren't qualified to be a wife; you will just be girlfriends, side-chicks, or part-time lovers. This is just a fact UNLESS you choose to develop wife skills and characteristics that will cause a man to see you in a different light. Your general behavior and attitude, as well as how you treat a man, will determine the category into which you fall. Anyone who wants to change can do so at any time with knowledge and application of that knowledge.

It bears repeating: You can't expect men to automatically see your value and choose you as a wife. Remember that in most cases, men weren't raised to know how to be a husband, or even a good mate. Since you are more of the nurturer by nature, PROJECT those skills to get him to understand what is expected of him and do it with the right spirit. This teaches your man how to be your husband.

Projection is even important after entering a relationship. I've been in and have witnessed many relationships where the love wasn't translating from one person to the other beyond just words. Over time, words that don't match real actions will eventually lead to a road of heartbreak, for one, if not both. This doesn't mean the love isn't present; it just means one party isn't translating their feelings into action. In commitments that last, action speaks far louder than words.

Ladies, you have more power than you know. You just tend to use it in a way that runs a man away versus turning him on and making him never want to leave. Projecting the "ME, ME, ME" thing works alright when dating for a little while, but it will fail you if you want to become a wife. If you burden a man with too much about you all the time, he will lose interest and eventually stop coming around. In a relationship, it must be "give and take", not a "take and take". Your projection creates his perception.

Prove that your presence and time are valuable and worth having for a lifetime. Everything you do should say, "I am marriage worthy, and you should choose me."

Chapter Sixteen

ARE YOU REALLY "WIFE" MATERIAL?

I believe most women have the potential to be a wife and mother. But, just because something is possible doesn't mean it needs to happen. Some of you ladies just aren't marriage material. Wanting to be a wife and possessing the necessary skill set are two different things. You get caught up in the infatuation of marriage, not realizing all that it entails. Men look for certain qualities in a woman when seeking a wife, and just having woman parts doesn't guarantee you a place in the running. Some of you simply don't have what it takes; the good news, however, is that if you want to, you can change.

Now, before you start doing your woman "reversal" thing, remember the point of this book. It's about why HE won't marry YOU! If you weren't curious about how to get him to choose you, you wouldn't be reading this book. Stay focused on that point and follow along. Again, this is not to say all men are husband material, so let's be very clear. That is another topic for another time. Male and female comparisons here skew the point I am trying to convey, so let's assume, in some statements, they are universal to both men and women. The focus here is YOU and why he won't marry you. Keep that in mind.

Ladies, do you possess basic wife skills? If not, are you willing to acquire them? Those things you learned almost from birth are some of them. Nurturing, caring, being supportive, being creative, and being willing to build that Dream House (remember Barbie and Ken?) are some qualities of a wife. For most men, sex is at the top of the list. But an extremely close second is cooking. Some men are better in the kitchen than women, so there are a few rare exceptions. But most men will tell you that a good wife is one who knows how to prepare decent meals to keep her man nourished and fed.

If cooking is not your strong suit, it's not too late to learn. These days, YouTube can teach you everything you need to know. Fast food and take-out are okay for the single life, but a man usually envisions home-cooked meals as part of the marriage package. The bottom line is that if you can take care of his stomach, his mind, and his penis, chances are you can keep him for good.

You must realize that when you want a man to ask you to be his wife, you are indirectly asking a hunter to stop hunting. That means the meal he gets called "you" needs to satisfy him for a lifetime. You'll need to know how to keep the party going. You must keep reinventing opportunity for that hunter to keep hunting you and only you. If you want him to stay loyal to you, you must continue doing what you did to get him to pop the question.

Sometimes, women get lazy after marriage. Some stop caring about their weight and appearance. Some stop keeping their hair up and lose the sexy underwear, replacing a nice hairdo with bonnets, and lingerie with flannel and slippers. Then kids enter the picture and time for bonding is compromised, as children become first priority in the home. Though life gets busy, the marital relationship needs continual investment.

If you haven't already done so, take time to watch the movie "War of The Roses." It's not uncommon for a woman to become bored and sometimes lethargic after she gets the ring, the house, and the kids. Getting a hobby or a job keeps women active and provides good motivation for maintaining a healthy and attractive appearance. It takes preparation and planning but maintaining your energy and your appearance as an individual benefits you, your marriage, and your family. Ladies, you need to understand this about being a wife.

If you keep a filthy home, or you put your own needs before your kids' needs, you are not wife material. He is looking for a woman who can not only take care of his needs, but who can manage a home and nurture and care for children. Messy women tend to end up being just sex partners, not wives. Always maintain a clean home, car, and appearance, as these things matter to a man. He wants to be able to bring you around his friends and family, so you must represent him well.

In marriage, "life" gets in the way. Sometimes plans get altered, jobs are lost, and family members die. Any life-changing event that affects either spouse will inevitably affect their marital relationship as well. A wife must be a "ride or die" type of woman. A wife navigates her family back to calmer waters by being the voice of stability and reason when life's storms hit. She's the one who keeps everything together when things seem to be unraveling fast. A wife is far greater than a girlfriend, as a girlfriend usually finds it hard to stay on the frontline of life with her man. A girlfriend has the option to bail when things get tough, but a wife is there for the long haul.

Your job as a potential wife is to show a man that you can be his everything, thereby eliminating his need for someone else. This is accomplished by showing him what you have to offer him for the long term. Remember, a man's initial reason for entering a relationship is to have fun. It's more casual for men at the outset, as they are still feeling you out and looking for qualities that say "long-term". Many women show men that they are merely a temporary stop to use for practice before getting with the woman worth marrying. Don't let that be you.

As a child, my parents told me not to get with a "ready-made family." In other words, they advised me to avoid all women who have children when considering a wife. Why did they teach me that? Because they wanted me to have my own family without dealing with what my potential mate did as a younger woman. Very often, women who have babies by several different men also have issues with them paying child support and being in their kids' lives. My parents didn't want me or my brothers to have to deal with "baby daddy" drama. They never wanted us to feel obligated to take on the responsibility of another man's kids before having children of our own.

Now, if you are one of these women, take no offense. There is a man out there for you; he just wasn't me. This in no way implies that you are not wife material, but it does limit your husband pool. Many men received the same advice from their parents that I got. As with all things, however, there are exceptions. Some single mothers find men who will take in their kids and their drama from past relationships and will thrive quite well. As a matter of fact, I know a woman who has 8 children and recently found love and got married. Mind you, if you saw her fine ass, you would think she had zero kids, but that is beside the point (insert laughter).

So, I'm not saying you women who have children won't find love or a husband. What I am saying is for every baby you have out of wedlock, to a man, you look like you have several bodies on you. No man wants to wife a woman who was considered the neighborhood whore. If everyone on the block hit it, no one on the block will wife it. No man wants to be out in the streets hearing about how other men ran all through you, and then come home and call you his wife. Whores want to be housewives, but men still see you as a whore. Realize that.

Women who've had children during a marriage, but later divorced or became widowed, are viewed a bit differently. They had a foundation for the birth of their children. Therefore, a potential suitor won't give them a wide side-eye for bringing kids into a new marriage. They've proven to the man they are wife material, as someone else chose to marry them in the past.

After all, he is looking for a woman who is interested in being a good mother as well as a wife.

Women in these circumstances have a good chance of marrying again, even with kids. Angel proved that, as she found the love of her life and married for a third time. Whether your kids are from a previous relationship or from a previous marriage, how you treat them will be a determining factor in whether the current beau will want to tie the knot; make no mistake about it.

Beautiful women with talent and wife skills will always have options. But, if you are a "baby's momma," please understand that every time you add a new last name to your offspring, you lose major points with men who perhaps would've chosen you as a wife. A woman's choices made while she is young will affect a man's choices when she is older. So, if you are one of my younger readers, or, if you have dating daughters, make them aware of this valid point.

Ladies, as a wife, you must be the backbone of your man, his strongest support system, his rock. You can't clutter the surface of your life with all your own baggage and expect a marriage to work. You are to be the strength and glue that binds the relationship. You will always do the most giving in the marriage because you were taught, from birth, to nurture; your man was not. He was taught to hunt, provide and protect. At times, he struggles with it, but a good wife knows how to get him back on his path to greatness.

A smart wife knows when to be assertive and when to be

submissive. The Bible speaks of submission, and women who claim to trust in it hate that word. Some feel it's a sign of weakness, which is funny to me. In reality, submission is a sign of strength. A woman who understands how the mind of a man works knows that submission to him is liberation for her. She's not submitting to his control or manipulation; she is submitting to his love and covering.

Ladies, you become that man's responsibility when you become his wife. So, listen to him, at least sometimes.

A wife is a source of comfort for a man. He battles with society, at the workplace, and with life all day. When he comes home, he expects comfort and solace, not a messy junkyard and a woman with a list of complaints. She is to be sensitive and appropriately responsive to his ups and downs, showing him love and encouragement, especially at his low points. These are the women men stay with for life.

A man wants a woman he can trust with his heart. He feels comfortable freely sharing every emotion when his wife creates a safe place for him to break down without feeling less than a man. I am a rare breed, as I have never had an issue with being forthright with my emotions. Boys are told to "Man up," when they get hurt. That makes no sense to a 10-year-old with a 5-inch gash in his arm, or to the 15-year-old, who's told to "Walk it off" when they have a fractured bone. They are taught to mask emotions, as crying around other boys is a sign of cowardice. Of course, in a boy's world, that could mean trouble.

Boys often conceal their feelings, carrying them well into

manhood. That makes it harder for men to express emotions without them turning into anger, the one emotion that's most acceptable in boyhood. But, a skilled wife takes interest in learning how to allow a hardened man space to let his feelings out. She lovingly lets him know it's okay to cry, and he's still her man. A man who is free with his emotions is easier to live with and more relatable.

Ladies, remember that you are experts at living in emotional spaces; for most men, however, it is awkward and uncomfortable. You sometimes expect us men to be more like you, which will never happen because we are simply wired differently. Once you accept this fact, it will be easier to fulfill your role as a wife.

Do you now understand what it means to be wife material? Unless you possess most of these qualities, you are not ready for marriage. These qualities will get a man's attention and get him in the door. If you want him to propose, learn how to become a wife now. Learn from wives of happy husbands and happy households. Learn from women who have been married for many years. They can help you develop into the wife any man would love to have.

Ladies, whatever you do, don't sell a man a dream you don't plan to fulfill. In other words, don't act like you are wife material when you know that you really aren't. You can't lie to him and get him on board, and then not fully commit to what you claimed you'd bring to the relationship. Just as you expect a man to fulfill every hope and dream he's given you as your future husband, he expects you to do the same as his future wife. Don't start out with lofty promises and get his hopes up only to become lax and detached from what you said. He will begin disrespecting you for selling him a dream that won't come true.

When you decide to change the terms of the relationship, you'd better also be ready to perform the tasks of your new station. If you know in your heart that you are not marriage-ready, don't sell a man fake hope to pressure him into a proposal. This will only create resentment. He's happy just sleeping with you, so don't manipulate him into going any farther than that.

Chapter Seventeen

YOUR BIOLOGICAL CLOCK IS YOUR PROBLEM, NOT HIS

The *biological clock* refers to a women's decrease in fertility with advancing age. Ladies are on a limited time for conceiving and bearing healthy babies. Men have no such deadline, as they can become fathers well into their 70's, or even later, with no risks. When the woman's biological clock starts ticking away, she knows that her window for having children is beginning to close. Consequently, she may become increasingly desperate to find a husband. Though her concern is understandable, this may create a burden for the men she dates, as she wants one of them to pop the question already! But this is the surest way to run any man off real fast.

For example, a woman in her mid-forties with no children may feel that her opportunity to experience motherhood is disappearing. She meets a man, and almost immediately, starts talking marriage and kids. He is not on her time, however, as they just met. The pressures of marrying her and having a child when he hasn't even known her long enough to decide if she's the one for him will make him very cautious. He'll likely feel the need to put the brakes on right away. Men don't like pressure, especially when it comes to lifetime plans like kids or marriage. They hate being coerced even when they are already married.

On a recent season of the Bravo reality series, *"Married to Medicine,"* cast member Lisa Nicole spent the entire season pressing her doctor husband to have a child. You could see the man was uncomfortable. But he wanted to make his wife happy, even though he had no interest in having a child at his age. Understanding that her desires were deep and real, however, Lisa's husband tried being supportive. As a doctor, his first concern was her health. He was also aware of the risks of having a stillbirth or deformed child. Lisa failed to realize that, even with a healthy birth and no complications, the prospect of another child would still have long-term implications for her husband.

He expressed his resistance to the idea clearly to other men; but he wasn't completely honest with his wife. The few times Lisa's husband tried to tell her his concerns that childbirth at her age would be a health risk, she wasn't hearing it. Even knowing she could die delivering a child, and even after all the doctors on the show told her the pros and cons, she was still hell-bent on having another baby. Her poor husband was really trying not to hurt her feelings, but if you saw the show, it was obvious that he didn't want a child at this juncture in his life.

Torn, Lisa's husband would eventually suggest a surrogate, to at least minimize the potential damage that could befall his awesome wife. But, make no mistake about it, he was opposed to the idea of having another kid. Yet, he wants his wife to be happy. What a dilemma. Love is an interesting drug.

Ladies, if you made the choice to put off having children until later in life, suddenly tuning in to the ticking of your "biological clock" will cause unwanted pressure in the relationship. This is especially true if your man is in his 40's and rejects the idea of parenting with you. Besides the risk of complications for both mother and child, you are asking him to father a child who will graduate from high school when he's in his 60s. YOU want him to be happy about the thought of a baby, but a new guy will think *Exit stage left!* An existing husband will hesitate in the sack.

Some women are so obsessed with this clock that nothing her potential baby's daddy says will change her mind. The man is probably thinking, *"What have I gotten myself into?"* She may be so focused on her childbearing expiration date, however, that she may not notice his hesitation. It's important for women to realize that this isn't his problem. And it's unfair to force parenthood on a man who may be done with raising kids.

Now, this is not to say that some guys won't buy in, but the probability is low unless a woman has already been with him for several years. However, a new guy will most likely run for the hills, and with good reason. He can see the focus is not on him or the relationship. The focus is on her own desire that she cannot accomplish without the donation of his sperm. Her desire is also time-based; so, she can't expect him to feel the love. All he feels is her fear of no longer being able to bear children.

This puts him in a situation where HE now is a victim of her biological clock.

Be mindful of the fact that most men up in age are not going to be on the same page with your biological clock. If you are fortunate to find one, or already have a mate that agrees with you, you are blessed. But, listen to him when he brings up facts about risk factors. Any loving man would advise you to consider the statistics before moving forward. Don't let the level of your focus on this particular goal supersede the focus of your current relationship with your man, and other life goals.

Ladies, remember the objective; you want this man to marry you. But, if at 45-50 years old he doesn't see himself as a new father, you will most likely lose him with talk about a baby. He is in the time of his life where he is expecting to get more into you and the relationship, not becoming a new parent. He wants to enjoy the next phase.

If you've already had children together that are now adults, he's probably now thinking, *"We can get back to our relationship as our kids are now fully grown."* Don't derail that plan just because your clock is ticking louder and louder in your head. The period of a safe and healthy delivery is rapidly diminishing. A man in love clearly has his wife's best interest at heart and will suggest other options. To her, it's *"You are not supporting me,"* but to him, it's *"I am trying to save your life and our relationship."*

Having kids should always be a joint decision. When an older woman is desperate to give birth, the man is often left out of the loop and the decision is between her and her body. While she nests up for another child like she is 25, he is slowly feeling as though his voice and his concerns don't matter. She is now controlling the entire relationship, and he has no say.

Ladies, if you are in a relationship that you want to lead to marriage, you have to remember that the man is also to be involved in major life decisions. Unlike you, the man is not under any emotional pressure. He will always come from a place of logic, not emotions. His opinion matters and is as valid as yours. Here is a good time to defer the situation to your man, whose stable mindset can give you realistic pro-versus-con options, or at least something else to consider. Trust his love for you, and his logic. Your emotions can run wild in the wrong direction.

The biological clock doesn't apply only to a woman's desire to have babies. It also applies to a woman's vision of just being married by a certain age. I know many women now approaching 50 years of age who say they are happy being alone. I can also often hear the bitterness and loneliness in the tone of their voice. They aren't saying they are happy being alone as much as they are mad they are alone. They blame their single status on the men who didn't commit to them. These women are up against their biological clocks as well but acting as if they don't care.

Ladies, you won't find love if you tell the men you meet, as well as everyone else, "I don't want or need a man," if in your heart, you really do. You deserve companionship but being bitter doesn't attract any quality of man into your life. Bitter, unhappy women are unattractive. Plus, you don't want to speak into your life what you don't really want. You shouldn't allow past failed relationships to stop you from opening your heart and mind to the possibilities of new love, regardless of your age. This part of your biological clock you can ignore, and you should. There is no age limit to finding love and happiness.

In all fairness, I am sure there are some men that may love you enough to say, "Let's go for it!" But, the closer you both get to 50, the chances of this happening get slimmer and slimmer, though not impossible. By the time we are in our fifties, we are all set in our ways and far more particular about what we like and dislike. Plus, women at midlife may begin to sense that most of the good men are already taken. The dating pool becomes sparse, though not completely empty. However, I still believe an open heart can find all the love it seeks at any age and at any time. The key is to be OPEN.

Ladies, your biological clock is never a man's issue; it's yours. Don't try to make it his issue either. It's only a turn-off. If he isn't ready to marry you, too much immediate pressure can scare him off. All a man sees is added stress. He might be polite about it when he's around you. He doesn't want to hurt your feelings, as this is a sensitive and emotional thing for you. But when you aren't around, he is telling all his male friends you are out of your mind.

Chapter Eighteen

FOR BETTER OR FOR WORSE

So many women allow past hurts to destroy future opportunities. Often, hurt people hurt people. Love, however, has neither boundaries nor timelines. Love can happen again at any time, so don't be this type of woman. Younger women need to exercise patience, and older women need to let go of old pains, allowing love an honest way back in. Allow past joys and pains to develop you into a more complete woman who is still open to building and growing with a man. Nothing from past relationships need be wasted.

Men have their issues from past relationships too. If you want a man to open up and be vulnerable, show him a little of your own vulnerability so he knows what it looks like. Any friend or woman can be there for a man when things are great, but where will you stand when things go south? The measure of any relationship is not how well you get along when you are winning and things are going great, but when you are falling, or have hit the bottom. Mature love can handle this very well.

Every relationship will be tested, and the way you manage the hard times will be its foundation. Fair-weather friends and iffy relationships come a dime a dozen, but a potential husband is seeking a potential wife, which means someone who is in it "for better or worse." A lot of women in this day and age don't accept that in life there will be seasons of "worse." Life is a series of events, some intense, tragic, and unforeseen. One's quality of life is determined by how those events are handled.

Ladies, your conflict-resolution skills, your ability to compromise, your ability to move on from pain, and your ability to love are the things that will get you to the next level with your man. Your biological clock issues and sulking about past relationship woes will take you backwards. If you feel the pressure of that clock, perhaps you need to take a step back and breathe. A man can't always be on the same page with you. Be willing to compromise if being with him means more to you than your personal agenda.

Remember, in marriage, it can't always be just about you. If you marry for the wrong reasons-- for money, for the sake of being married, for fear of growing old alone, or just to get a man to father a child legitimately--your marriage won't survive. It has no solid foundation. Love is the only real reason to ever marry, as material things will come and go, and conditions are subject to change. But love never fails.

Ladies, if you are up in age but want to become a wife and new mother, all hope is not gone. It's just important that you only invest your time into a man who wants the same. If you are both in agreement on this issue, there will be no pressure. If you are already married and are a mother of older children, don't pressure your husband at this stage of your lives to have another baby if he doesn't want one. It's more feasible to consider bonding with each other, traveling, and having fun by yourselves.

Chapter Nineteen

GET YOUR BITTER, SINGLE FRIENDS OUT OF YOUR EAR

Another deathblow to a man's interest in you is your single, bitter, man-less friends. You know the ones I'm talking about; the ones who've had messed up relationships and are now miserable. You shoo-shoo with them about problems with your man, and they respond with, *"Girl, if it was me, I wouldn't take that shit."* She then loads the conversation with bad advice. Your vulnerable state allows her garbage to seep into your failing relationship.

Wake up, ladies! If they can't hold a man, why would you let their toxic ideas enter your head? Do you really think they care about you and your love life when they are bitter about their own? My ex once said to me, "I had my girls in my ear." I said, "Well, how did that work out for ya? This is why you have "EX" attached to your name in our relationship." Sure, your friends wouldn't take what you've tolerated, and that is why your friends are home alone with D batteries complaining to you, with the intent of having you home alone too. Misery loves company. Those are not the friends with whom you need to share your relationship business. You must be very careful.

Believe it or not, most of your girlfriends don't mind seeing you happy, provided they experience that desired happiness FIRST. When you're in love, some of your friends hate it because it takes away from your girlfriend time with them. Your loneliest friend doesn't want to see you marry before her. And, if she is devious enough, she may even secretly try to encourage you to destroy what you have with your man. Therefore, her advice should be taken with a grain of salt. It clearly got her a spot on the couch alone. Do what she did, and you will get what she got. You too can start complaining about how messed up men are as you share the couch and ice cream with this pathetic "friend" you thought had your back. What a sad scene.

Now watch what happens as soon as a dude pays the slightest attention to your lonely friend. She will lose that negative talk and bail on you to spend more time with him. She will have just put you on the couch alone, while she is now back on the prowl. The objective is to beat you to happiness so she isn't alone, even if it means ditching you. Sounds crazy, but this happens all the time.

If you wish to keep your man, keep your personal business out of the ears of your girlfriends. Confiding in single women who are mad at men could be the death of your relationship. If you need someone to confide in, find a happily married friend and open up to her, as she will give you sound advice. Successfully married women know what it takes to maintain a healthy relationship. They won't encourage you to do things that will backfire with your man. They can also teach you better ways to communicate with him.

Bella listened to her bitter, single friends and to one of her married friends whose trucker husband was rumored to have slept around on her. Thus, Bella absorbed both single and married bitterness, and consequently, this affected me. She let their opinions about our relationship affect her movement with me. Now those same friends are happy, but she is alone again. Angel was just the opposite, as she never cared what other people thought. I knew her mother and sons, and we all interacted well. I would even dare to say, at times, they were like family.

If you want a husband, don't listen to those cackling, lonely women you call "friends." Following their advice will only set your relationship up for a massive failure. Always be discerning when it's necessary to share your problems. Know what to share and what not to. Use discretion and take into account their trustworthiness. There are great men open to spending a lifetime with a good woman, but a good woman is wise enough to keep her friends out of her love life.

Marriage isn't about finding the right person. It's about BECOMING the right person. Be someone who attracts a man that will desire a lifetime of memories with you. Don't let others' failed relationships rob you of your chance at lasting love.

Chapter Twenty

THE CEREMONY IS ALL ABOUT YOU

Though it may be every woman's childhood dream to have a "Kim Kardashian" wedding, a man couldn't care less. Understand that the entire marriage ceremony is more about you than him and is rooted in your childhood fantasies. Your fiancé is already very aware of this and is totally fine with it. If you don't believe me, let me break it down for you.

You get an expensive, one-of-a-kind, Vera Wang dress that you will never wear again in your life. Then it's the dope new designer shoes, the hair, the nails and the feet. Then, there's the huge bridal party that you spent months hand-picking, along with their dresses (that aren't as hot as yours, of course), your choice of food, the cake, the theme, and the colors. Oh! And let's not forget that you get a new diamond ring. So, this wedding is all about you. It's fulfilling a dream that you've had all your life. Still not convinced? Let's review what he gets.

The man's input is asked only because you want to appear to involve him. So, you act as if some things are a joint decision. He gets to taste several different cake samples, but none are the one you choose. He is just foil in the planning process. He gets a few of his male friends to say they will walk down the aisle with YOUR friends. He rents a tuxedo that some kid threw up on while wearing at the prom two days prior along with matching rental shoes. He gets a gold band sans diamonds that he didn't help pick, and about which he does not really care. And, he gets the same haircut he's gotten for the last 4 years from the same barber. His only bright spot is his bachelor party, which puts you both on even ground since you will have a bachelorette party. So, in comparison, the wedding ceremony is clearly all about you.

With this said, you should consider the cost of impressing a bunch of people who couldn't care less if your marriage survives. Wedding expenses start most newlyweds off in a lot of debt. Debt, especially in the early stages of marriage, creates problems. I know many divorced people who are still paying for the wedding! So, dial back a bit on the "dream wedding," and be smart about finances for the long term.

Excessive debt is one of the main causes of relationship breakdowns. And this brings me to my next point.

Ladies, comfort and security are both top priorities for most of you. Don't allow financial pressure to force you to compromise these priorities. When marrying, you're giving yourself to the man who is to honor you and collaborate with you in building a life. But money woes are the first layer of decay that starts the breakdown in communication and causes each party to stop doing the things that made them marry in the first place. Financial trouble creates a chain reaction. Frustration leads to bad communication, which leads to neglect, which opens the door for potential infidelity, which could lead to a total break-up. Be careful of how far you go to impress a bunch of friends and family.

My wife and I thought it was a wise choice to go to Vegas to tie the knot. We spent a whopping $150 and have been married 26 years. My friends Byron and Mylette Nora took it a step further and re-married us on our first anniversary so friends and family could attend. We did it African-style, as Mylette is a wardrobe stylist. She made African garb for both of us, and we even jumped the broom. It was a surprise wedding! So, I married the same women twice for a total of $150 dollars. And we are still together today.

Marriage is not about other people; it's about the two of you. Don't try to impress everyone by spending money you don't have. The crowd will be gone once the wedding is over. You begin living together as husband and wife the day you say, "I do." Even though this day is the fulfillment of your bridal dreams, keep your husband and the days beyond the ceremony in mind.

Chapter Twenty-One

AFTER HE TAKES THAT KNEE

So, you managed to get this guy to ask, "Will you marry me?" You've finally gotten that ring you've been dreaming of for years. Congratulations! But what happens after you get the ring? This is where the real work starts. Getting married is not like winning the jackpot. The most important work starts AFTER you say, "I do," not before. So, let's discuss what it now takes to keep your new husband.

Once there is no more pinnacle to reach, I have seen many women just get plain lazy. Everything is anti-climactic. All the cool things they did to get that man locked in start to quickly go away. The sexy Victoria's Secret outfits are put away until special occasions, the hair is rarely done, the flannel comes out and the weight comes on. She cooks and cleans less and less. Now that she thinks she has nothing else to work hard for, the relationship, over time, becomes stale.

Sex is now used as a weapon on "mad" day, and arguments have become the norm. Two people who were once excited about this union are now looking at each other like *"What the hell was I thinking!"* Add in kids, and the sex life now has to be scheduled. Responsibilities, bills, and stress come to the forefront of their lives, and they now must work hard to keep this thing together. All the excitement they once shared comes to a screeching halt. He gets to see what she really looks like around the house, without the make-up and hair intact. The active love and caring is replaced with resentment and anger. The magic wears off. But why is that? Isn't this what they both wanted? Absolutely not!

When the man signs up for this task, he does it because he thinks all that fire and passion he and his new wife had together will remain. He believed she would still do the things she did to get him but is now learning otherwise. He starts to show less interest and she eventually does the same. The problems in the relationship become bigger than the reason they got married in the first place. Love will make him look past some changes, but over time, he starts to feel his wife has nothing else to work for. She is now becoming complacent in the relationship.

This isn't to say that men don't do the same because some do. But ladies, you control a lot of where your relationship goes once it's official. You actually have this power. Thus, when you start changing, he will do the same. Most men will tell you they want things to be the way they were. But with mounting bills, kids, and new job responsibilities, the relationship starts to fall apart. It's just a new reality for them to factor in and work on.

We've already established that the wedding was the fulfillment of a childhood fantasy. You both, as husband and wife, need to understand that the real work begins after the wedding ceremony. He agreed to the dream wedding you always wanted; but now, he needs you to agree to be the wife that helps fulfill the dream life he wants with you. Each of you must uphold your end of the deal to be everything you can to and for each other. This makes life continue to feel the way it did before marriage.

Some people are lucky. I have a few friends that made their marriages work for decades. I am on year 26 myself, and I had a good example. My mother and father were together for 54 years, until death parted them when my mother passed on my wife's birthday, May 11th, 2015. I had the pleasure of seeing how a relationship survived highs and lows by simply growing up in my parents' home. (Oddly enough, my parents' names are Abraham and Sarah, although we weren't very active in church. But I digress.)

The point here is that I had the opportunity to see a relationship work, though my wife didn't. Her example was a bit different from mine. Her parents divorced when she was still a child. Both had moved on to other relationships, but never remarried. When we argued, (and yes, you will argue), she was always quick to say, "Well let's end it." But I always said, "Let's work it out." Our responses to problems were based on what each of us saw while growing up. Believe it or not, what you witness between your parents will shape how you deal with your own marriage.

If you had the privilege of seeing a marriage work, you have something on which to base your perseverance. On the other hand, if you never saw one work, you have something on which to base your fears and your failures. However, every married couple has problems, regardless of the examples they witnessed. The couples that survive deal with their issues head-on, and those that don't simply fall apart. This is where all that love you both have deep down inside for each other must surface. Maybe you felt it best while you were still dating. Once you are married, however, you need to draw on that love to help you through challenging times.

What is the purpose of coming so far if you don't plan on making it work? Both parties must find a way to communicate on issues and work on them together. Don't let the frustrations of life put division between you and your mate. Be willing to work out your differences with love and care. Remember, there are others who are available outside of your marriage, and they would love to step in and make matters worse for both of you.

Married people are attractive to single people. Both men and women see a married person as someone who can commit. Don't think for a second that, just because you are married, outsiders won't try to get with one, if not both of you when they see an opening due to your unhappiness. The same tenacity that brought this thing together must be present to keep it together. You can never get too comfortable in marriage assuming that your spouse is immune to cheating. Boredom, neglect, and disrespect will easily set up situations that bring you back to the dating scene, as one or both are now looking for that feeling in someone new that is now lost in your own relationship.

To keep your man, you must be willing to do what you did to get him. This routine is non-stop if you want him to remain faithful. If your man likes your size, try your best to maintain it. If he likes you in sexy things, wear sexy things. A man will start to lose interest when you stop doing the things you did to lock him down. He starts to feel duped, used, and played, and he will surely start cheating on you. That's a promise.

A man wants the same feeling that got him to jump the broom. Now, of course he understands a few things will change as you are in it for life. But when you lose the core things that made you both want each other, the contract called "marriage" becomes nothing more than that: a contract. The loyalty and love attached to it can very easily dissolve if you don't continue working to maintain it.

Think of your relationship as a beautiful flower. You must feed it, water it and talk to it for it to grow. It needs the right mix of sunlight and darkness to flourish. Balance your relationship the same way. You must put even more time into it after you get married than when you were dating. You can't get lazy after he commits, as carelessness and complacency are usually the death of all unions. Once the knot is tied, the investment must continue.

Marriage is not a show for others, but a COVENANT between you and your husband. It needs to be treated with love, care, and respect. Being a wife is more than just something you use to impress your girlfriends and family. Some of you love to pose staring at your ring like you're in a Mannequin Challenge, showing off for your friends. But you must realize it's a lifetime job that extends even into seasons of tough times. It's during those times when both parties must work the hardest to keep it alive. Keep in mind that your marriage is not a tabloid story for your bored and lonely friends, so keep your hardships to yourselves.

Being a wife involves far more than just being someone's girlfriend. You are legally agreeing by contract to build your lives together in the eyes of God and all of society. As a wife, you must be willing to stand in the trenches with your man and family, during the brightest highs and darkest lows. Any woman not fully-committed to this concept doesn't need to force any man to marry her. Just continue dating, as it is less responsibility for those who can't handle it. Again, marriage is not for everyone.

A man will tell you what he wants and likes. As his wife, he expects these things from you. You have to make the time to keep it hot in both the bedroom and in daily life or you will watch your marriage end in a divorce. A man gets really turned off when he takes himself off the market to commit to you and then you suddenly get lazy in the marriage. You'd feel the same if he slacked in being your hero and protector.

Ladies, don't expect your man to automatically know everything about you, but rather show him how you wish to be treated, as all women are not the same. Every man should take the time to learn the woman he is with. What worked for previous lovers may not work for you, so it's on you to show him what is effective where you are concerned. And, it's on him to listen and comply the same way he wants you to comply with his wishes. This is work, but the reward is an enjoyable marriage.

Marriage is not a 40-yard dash. It's a marathon, then a decathlon. It's to be a lifetime situation that short-term people just need to avoid. Marriage is the ultimate sacrifice of self, as you are now responsible for supplying someone else's wants and needs, and for helping them with their dreams and goals. Marriage is not for people who fight for power; controlling another grown-up is not a realistic goal. There is no room for selfishness as you are now a part of a union, a team. A man wants a woman to hold him, not hold him down.

Respect is a major component in any relationship, and a marriage requires twice as much of it. It's huge, and for men, it's an actual need. If you don't want him to yell at you, you might not want to yell at him. Resist the temptation to make sarcastic, insulting, or belittling remarks, even if such remarks are intended in fun. Even if you are only joking, he won't experience it that way.

Avoid any "humor" that he might experience as a put-down. Regardless of modern-day gender norms, the reality is that he needs to be viewed as "the man." When you treat him as such, you will know for certain, in front of all your friends and family, that you are "the woman" for him. And that comes with much reward; I guarantee it. Don't let a bad attitude destroy your future with someone you love.

If you wish to keep your marriage forever, never forget

what you did to make him ask for your hand. You must exude and maintain the same level of love, affection, caring, and attentiveness that made him decide you were "the one." If you were the right woman then, you are the right woman now; never forget that. Don't lose focus of your objective now that you got the prize. Nurture it, build it and respect it. It's your marriage.

Chapter Twenty-Two

YOU'VE GOT DADDY ISSUES

Through no fault of your own, too many of you grew up without the affirmation of your father. This void in your life may have kept you from fully trusting men. As a result, some of your "daddy" issues impede your ability to have healthy interaction with a man who truly loves you. I've encountered women whose fathers failed them. Consequently, they were incapable of showing love, but were masters at receiving it. These encounters left me drained because I was doing all the giving, which was never really appreciated anyway. They kept me emotionally bankrupt because what I gave was never enough.

The absence of a father in a girl's life is deeply painful and may impact her relationships with males well into her adulthood. This is a real issue that should be dealt with professionally. If this was your experience, you might consider doing the work necessary to heal, as this is hard to fix on your own. Your father's absence from your life was not your fault; but your emotional well-being is your responsibility.

If you are a woman who missed out on enjoying a healthy

relationship with your father, you may find yourself trying to pull a "father" out of every man you date. You expect a man to make up for what you needed, but never received, from your dad. The problem is that a man doesn't want to be your daddy. He wants to be your lover. He can't and won't be both. Yet, if the void in you is that intense, you will unknowingly put pressure on him that he can't handle. His visits will become fewer, and phone calls increasingly scarce. If he is a sensitive man, he won't want to hurt your feelings. So, to avoid the pressure, he will just gradually disappear. If this has happened repeatedly, it may be the reason that your relationships don't last.

Let's go back a bit to sex. Calling a man "daddy" or "papi" when his manhood is deep inside you is just plain weird. To you, it sounds strong, like you are passing the power of command to him; but when he is being passionate, and you scream "Daddy!", he thinks you have a sexual attraction to your father, which is kind of creepy when you think about it. Remember, this is HIS perception of what you are PROJECTING.

Half of sex is mental. When you call your man anything referencing a father, you imply that he needs to be a different type of provider for you than just being your lover. If he called you "Mom" or "Mother" as he stroked you repeatedly in the bedroom, you would understand how an *"Oedipus Complex,"* works. By definition, *Oedipus Complex* means "a desire for sexual involvement with a parent of the opposite sex, and a concomitant sense of rivalry with a parent of the same sex."

Let that sink in.

Calling your man "Daddy" in bed or otherwise sets up a dynamic that will have him talking to you like a child later. And, I know you don't want that. In fairness, some couples enjoy the use of this word, as it is playful and makes the man feel somewhat empowered. I personally find it uncomfortable in sexual moments; as uncomfortable as one would be having sex with a picture of their mother or grandmother facing them. Ewww.

I would also challenge the women who call their men "Daddy" on a regular basis to review how he speaks to them on mad day. Is his authoritative? Only you would know. Just like some say, "You are what you eat," many would also say, "You speak your realities into existence."

A husband is not your father. "Daddy" implies he fills the void of a man who created you, implying he is responsible for you the child, not you the adult.

Chapter Twenty-Three

HE NEEDS YOUR SUPPORT

Men like myself are independent contractors, so we don't work normal jobs. When not acting, I create shows, write and produce movies, and run a film production company. Those of us who work in the entertainment industry, or similar professions, love women who can step into the empire we're building for "us" and assist. If you're married to this type of man, but you constantly complain about the work he puts in trying to build a future for the family, you are viewed as opposition to what brings him joy. That's a huge turn-off. What made me love Jennifer is she understood what it would take for me to make it to the top of my profession. She didn't get in the way of my goals and pursuits as she knew that she, our children, and my nearest kin would reap the benefits.

Ladies, you shouldn't try to usurp attention from your man's personal goals, as these were already in place when you met him. You should try to have a PART in his goals and prove by your actions that you are in his corner and on his team. And, if your skill set simply cannot help with the growth of his business, the least you can do is not stand in the way of his success. Just being supportive works well too. He isn't doing this just for him anymore; he is now also doing it for you.

While in college, I told my wife-to-be that my career was my number-one priority, and if she ever got in the way of it, we were done. She heard me, moved me to California, got a job at a talent agency, and got my voice career off the ground. Instead of slowing me down or getting in the way, she became a vital part of my success. This is the kind of wife a man wants and needs.

A supportive wife holds her man's attention when she helps him obtain his goals. This is what he looks for when considering a woman to be his wife. On the other hand, the chick that bitches because he's in the studio late will make him want to spend the night there. Complaining about his business travel will make him eager for the next trip.

If your man's aspirations require long hours away from home, you must be secure enough to trust that he's doing what he feels he must to reach his goals. Show that you are secure and supportive, not insecure, jealous, and demanding. Be the woman he can't wait to get home to, and with whom he will want to continue a long-term relationship.

If your man has an entertainment or athletic career that keeps him in the public eye, he may be desirable to masses of women. Now, a slight tad of jealousy is normal as it is an indication of your desire to safeguard the exclusive bond you have with the one you value and cherish. But when it becomes insane and starts bleeding out like a monthly cycle, it is time to reassess it to determine its level of detriment to the relationship. A little jealousy is sometimes even cute, but when it affects a man in making his coins, exhibiting too much will run him off.

I have seen many cases, some even on reality shows, where a woman is insanely jealous of the time her man puts into his career goals. If she is not trying to assist him in his pursuits, she certainly doesn't need to become the speed bump in front of his goals. That's how men end up hating their women, making even a post-breakup friendship out of the question. No man wants an excessively jealous woman any more than a woman wants an excessively jealous man. It can become cruel and destructive beyond repair. Your husband should be your best friend if you wish to survive until death do you part. It starts with supporting each other in every way possible.

Chapter Twenty-Four

MASTER DEBATING

Lovers fight. Even in healthy relationships, there are disagreements, some of them intense. Women tend to fight from a place of emotion, while men fight from a place of logic. You can't argue emotions, as they are subjective and differ according to the person and the offense. However, you can debate facts and logic, as these are universally understood--or, at least they should be.

Just an FYI: A man gets hella frustrated when he has to deal with a lot of off-subject arguing. You have to stay focused on the conversation at hand. I have had hundreds of social media debates with women who won't adhere to the subject. They also post off-topic questions to which they don't really want answers. Why ask questions if all you plan to do is answer them yourself? If you already know all the answers, you can stop asking questions.

During my chats with women, I tried to give direct answers, but they immediately refuted what I said without giving it any thought. I'm thinking, *"Hey Boo, if you know every damn thing, date yourself. Why am I even in this conversation?"*

When a man sees you really don't care for his opinion, he will stop offering it.

Another tactic I've seen is that women will sometimes take what a man says, personalize it, and then reverse it on him. This is a sign of an emotionally needy woman who just wants attention. Ladies, this is not the way to get it. All this does is push men away, as they begin to realize their opinions or responses aren't really valued.

When a man talks, he expects you to listen objectively without making more or less of what he says. And, when you don't understand what he says, he expects you to ask him for clarity before you react negatively. Don't make conversing with you so difficult that he saves it for another woman who's willing to listen.

I understand that you ladies often only want to give your opinions in conversations. No real man will tolerate that, especially when you get loud and defensive. To him, you sound like a nagging mother. And no grown man wants to be taken back to boyhood stage. If you start yelling like he's a child, you make zero sense to him. He just sees that your emotions are all over the place. Not only are your points unclear, you're also rejecting anything he says, which tells him you take yourself far too seriously. Rather than draw him toward you, your emotional outbursts will only push him out the door. Again, you must think of your objective.

A home is a place for a man to relax, not be combative. So, don't turn the atmosphere in your home into a war zone. Choose your battles, because not all are worth fighting. Most women have issues with this because they often feel they need to get things off their chest. Unloading your dissatisfaction onto a man will likely make him feel cornered and attacked. First, assess where he is emotionally before you come in with the heavy artillery. He may have some outside pressures that will cause him to blow up on you if your approach is wrong or poorly timed.

If you ask a man something, accept his answer even if you don't agree with it or like it. You don't have to like it, but not accepting it forces him to feel what you don't want him to feel: DISRESPECTED. A man needs respect and will hang out wherever he's getting it. Your man feels respected when he is heard, when his opinions are valued, when his feelings are acknowledged, and when your communication with him affirms his dignity. Respect him enough to hear what he has to say if you don't want him to stray.

Some women think that a man is supposed to share in her feelings about certain situations but can't understand why he doesn't. Just know he also can't understand why you think he should. Logic tells him that whatever the situation may be isn't that serious, regardless of what you think. Accept that he is entitled to feel what he feels; otherwise, the message you send is that you're not letting up until he changes his tune. This is a guaranteed recipe for conflicts. He is not you and will not always empathize with you or see things through your eyes. So, don't try to make the impossible happen, as you are not God.

He has just as much right to his feelings as you do to yours.

If you want to avoid unnecessary fights, timing is important. If you want your man to do something for you, you must know when to ask him. If he just walked in the door from a long and exhausting day at work, that's not the time to ask him for anything. I don't care how long it's been on your mind. If you approach him then, your results may vary depending on the man, but they won't be good. However, if you wait until he has eaten and is relaxed, especially after some good sex, chances are you will get exactly what you want and more. Men are more willing to hear you when they feel satisfied in one of these areas. You don't want to dump on a man who is tired, hungry, or sexually frustrated.

Ladies, you need to know how to effectively communicate what you want to a man to get results. For starters, talk to him, not AT him; his responses to you will be less defensive. Get out of your feelings and on to your objective, which is to get your way. There's nothing wrong with trying to get your way. But, you won't get it by being overbearing or forceful with him. Be a wise woman and cleverly make him feel your request was his idea. Learn persuasion because it's far more effective than shaking your finger in his face and ordering him around.

Men really aren't complicated; sometimes, however, you ladies make things complicated unnecessarily. Try keeping things simple and learn to communicate without heightened emotions. Men don't respond well to excessive drama, as it just puts them on the defense. Let me remind you that boys are brought up to be aggressive, protective, and reactive. Don't challenge him too much while communicating, as you could get your feelings hurt. He will revert to his natural instincts and not see you as the woman he really loves.

If you want your relationship to be successful and peaceful, you must master the art of debating with a man by learning to listen, by showing respect, and by remaining calm.

Chapter Twenty-Five

TRUST IS A MUST

One of the worst things you could ever do is embarrass your man in public. This includes sharing pillow talk with your girls, private information which could end up in the streets. Once it's out there, you can't retrieve it.

One of the problems I had in my marriage was my wife's childhood friend. I never got along with this woman. Every time she came around before my wife and I got married, she always created friction in our developing relationship. She always wanted to do a "double date" with my then girlfriend, but I was never invited. This happened when she visited her family in my hometown of New Orleans, and happened more often when we moved to California, where they both grew up. They often left me at home with my girlfriend's dad, as they hung out at TGI Friday's. They called it "ladies night" to justify why I was never invited. This happened almost every weekend, as she and her childhood crew hung out like old times.

Now, here's the offensive part. She would come home and tell me that Sherice was there with her boyfriend Chris, and Vida was there with her guy, Monty. The justification was that they all went to grade school together and were always tied at the hip. Needless to say, this only increased my dislike and distrust of her childhood friend, as she never saw it from my point of view. Her single friend, who doesn't like me, is keeping me on the couch while she hangs with her and other guys. Even worse, my girlfriend supported it. Each week, I would be left behind while hearing about couples in the crew that had more respect for their mates than she had for me.

The bond Jennifer shared with this particular woman was offensive to me because whenever the two of them were together, she was a different person. While hanging with this woman, my girl's phone suddenly never worked. They were always out with a bunch of men, all of whom her friend referred to as "cousins." I had to ask, "How many male cousins does this broad have? You grew up with her, so you know they aren't her family. Why is it that every time you are with this woman, everything you do is always suspect?"

I can tell a million stories on this subject, but suffice it to say, some of your friends can be detrimental to your relationship. Things I shared in confidence in my home after we got married ended up in salons in Los Angeles. When I heard them, I knew the only person I shared them with was my wife. Jennifer believed this friend would be loyal and could be trusted, even though this woman is known for repeating everyone's business. Her best friend was "The Mouth of the South;" yet, Jennifer thought what she confided in this woman would stay just between the two of them. Come on now! It doesn't take a rocket scientist to figure out who's the mole!

When you betray your man, he won't trust you, and will tell you less and less. To this day, because of this woman and their close relationship, even my wife isn't informed of everything I do or think. I won't open the door for her to cry on this chick's shoulder again when she knows she doesn't like me. More importantly, I won't allow her to slander my name, as she was never a fan. Why would she be? Jennifer didn't pick a husband from their circle of friends, so they can't double-date as they'd dreamed of doing as kids.

While sharing everyone's business like an unwanted blog, my wife's friend is damn near 50 years old with no kids and no ring. And it will probably remain that way for her. This is the albatross type of friend that wants to mess up everyone else's relationships because she never had one of her own to last. This woman is so up in everyone else's business because she doesn't have enough business of her own. Sad, to say the least.

Think about it. If a half-century has passed and no one has put a ring on her hand, she is not wife material. So, why would my wife really think this friend of hers cares whether our relationship works? Hell no! She needs my wife to run with her like old times, with no respect for our marriage.

You can't tell these types of women your problems. They are selfish and want you to die old, lonely and miserable like them. I can't tell you how much this damaged my marriage and my ability to trust. Recovering from this situation wasn't easy at all.

Now, I won't sit here and act like I didn't do some dirt inside my marriage. I am far from innocent, but when the wife puts it out there, it is instantly accepted as truth and tends to go viral. What she forgives, others won't live down. As this is how gossip works in the industry, who's to say the lull in my career wasn't due to the mess being spread in every salon in LA? Only God knows. My wife provided the ammo to a person she knows doesn't like me; hence, trust was broken on both sides for totally different reasons.

You women need to learn from the school of Hillary Clinton. After Bill Clinton was accused of having sex with Monica Lewinski, Hilary kept silent. Now, I know some of you think *"I would have raised all sorts of hell;"* but she was smart. She was planning to run for president in a few years and didn't need to be bitter about it publicly. Don't think for a second Bill didn't get an earful and made some serious *"I will support you when you run for President"* promises in their bedroom. The world waited to hear Hillary break down and cry, but she kept it all tight-lipped to the point where we will remember her Presidential run more than his infidelity.

In the face of public adversity and humiliation, Hillary Clinton kept the home life private, and she and Bill are still married to this day, though it was an embarrassing situation. Men will do stupid stuff at times, but his strength is in his wife's strength. Don't give people your business to run in the ground. Whatever the issue is, you need to resolve it with your mate, not your single, lonely hater friends. Keeping your business within the home creates a safe space and proves to your man that he can trust you with his mistakes, his feelings, his thoughts, and his vulnerability.

A final point about trust: Never let a man learn from someone else what you should have told him yourself. He doesn't appreciate second-hand information about you from an outsider. You can't possibly expect him to want you as his life-partner when others are privy to facts about you that he should have. It's better to risk making him angry or hurting him with your honesty than it is to risk compromising trust because of your dishonesty. Deception never wins.

Chapter Twenty-Six

REAL LOVE IS WITHOUT CONDITIONS

L adies, you don't want conditional love, so why give it? If your love comes with conditions, you are not marriage material. Love should be without limits; otherwise, it's just not real love.

Conditional love is like alternative facts; it's just straight-up fake. There is a huge difference between loving someone unconditionally and loving someone only when things are favorable and unchallenged. Learn the difference. I don't care how fine you are, how pretty you are, or what you are putting out under the sheets. A relationship built on conditional love won't last because it has no real substance or firm foundation from which to blossom. Unconditional love must be the foundation and it must go both ways.

I've dated women in the past whose love came with conditions--restrictions, negotiations, bargains, and self-serving limitations. Hence, I never considered any of them for marriage. These women usually had daddy issues, man issues, trust issues, or had been hurt so often they could neither receive nor give love freely in return. You could shower these women with love; beyond their words, however, they were just unable to give it back. Their actions never matched their words. These are the types of women who will also say all the right things but will justify their negligence with a bunch of excuses. As it is with you, men don't want to hear your excuses. If you say it, do it, or just don't say it at all. He is expecting you to keep your word on all things as you are expecting the same from him.

Bella was one who had this issue, big time. She was the queen of broken promises. She was a perpetual "promise and letdown," but would always want to argue with me because I called her out on her failure to follow through. She would say things like, "Money can't buy what we have." But, every time she failed on a promise and I confronted her on it, she'd deny it, and then break up with me. People who break up at every fight are not marriage material. Their so-called "love" can't be trusted.

One of the purposes of becoming a union is to weather storms together. Women like Bella see a storm and flee. No man is going to see a wife in a woman who does that. That shows him that she will be neither dependable, nor accountable for her behavior in the relationship. I will bet anything that this woman will die alone because she runs every time a man gets too close, all the while demanding more closeness and making little time to experience it.

Men see women like Bella as "fun only." He can't build a future with a woman who doesn't own up to her mistakes or make things right in a timely fashion. Women like her do nothing but make men mad at the next woman, because they wasted so much of his time playing games. Bella was one of several women I would have considered marrying. But, of all on my list, she was the least qualified because of her irresponsibility and her need to demand more while giving less. She was generally disinterested in helping me build my career, although I took time to help her build hers. She was incapable of unconditional love.

A man wants a woman who can love him, no matter what. Save the ultimatums and *"I'm leaving you"* threats. You can't push for a marriage in just words, but not show your man you really want it by your actions. That sends him mixed messages, and eventually, will make him more of an enemy to you than a friend. You can spend time loving the IDEA of marriage, but if you don't understand the reality of it and do the work, it will always elude you. That's why Bella is currently in her late 40s, still sexy, and still very single. Go figure.

Bella, it turns out, was selfish and deceptive for a very good reason. Hindsight is 20/20, and looking back, I thank God that the future I once imagined with her was not to be. When she left me, word was that she was embarrassed for dating a married man. Little did I know, however, that I was not her only lover. The real love of Bella's life was her boyfriend of over 20 years, a noted "pharmaceutical representative" who lived in another state. She was dating us both, although I knew nothing about him. I must say, she did a good job keeping that under wraps.

During our affair, she even had the audacity to confront my wife to ask if we were still intimate, all the while knowing she had a long-time relationship with this guy. Ironically, her beau resembled the type of character that I've often portrayed in movies. Perhaps she was attracted to me in the first place because she confused my film persona with my real character. (I chuckle every time I read this part.)

With my marriage and her long-distance lover, our affair was destined to dead-end. While I was completely honest with her about my wife, she kept me in the dark the entire time about the other man. Once she fell in love with me, she couldn't figure out how to balance her new feelings against the old flame she kept burning in secret. I will give her credit for ending our relationship before I learned of his existence.

I thank God for helping me dodge that bullet. I was about to ruin my life with a woman who had "Jeffery Dahmer" levels of deception in her character. After having experienced REAL LOVE with my wife, I am so grateful that I learned to recognize the fake.

True love is free of fear. When a woman has been hurt and is afraid of being hurt again, she may erect protective barriers around her heart. She may focus most intently on preserving herself above all else. I believe in self-love, but some women live in a place of hurt, and the walls they create become almost impossible for a good man to break through. This is a form of self-sabotage, preventing her from loving and being truly loved. Sad as it sounds, it is true. Even worse, women will still marry knowing they have these unresolved issues. It won't work.

Without unconditional love, don't expect your marriage to last. Anyone can say the words, "I do," but not all can keep the "Till death do us part" intact. Unconditional love is the key here. If you have conditions for your love as his wife, you will resort to them when you aren't getting your way. Why should a man waste his time building a life with you if he can't count on your stability? It's just a matter of time, and your services will no longer be needed.

The other woman is everything to the man who's been neglected. So, don't get mad when she gains his attention. Whatever it is that he likes or needs that you won't do, I promise you, someone else will. If she is stable and dependable and you aren't, don't be surprised when he prefers her over you. Ultimately, he has to think of his needs when selecting a long-term mate. So, not meeting them is how you become an "ex."

Conditional love has no place in any serious relationship on any level. No man willingly chooses to marry a woman whose commitment to him is unsure. If she does get so lucky, it won't last. In time, he will see the love has limitations and "fine print." He will surely stray to find someone who will show that she cares consistently about his wants, needs, dreams, and aspirations. Be the woman who supports her man and loves him no matter what. This is what a husband seeks in his wife. This is the woman he will find it hard to walk away from.

Chapter Twenty-Seven

HE DOES NOT WANT TO MARRY HIS MOTHER

A man may be attracted to a woman with similar qualities as his mother. After all, she is the first woman who ever showed him unconditional love. He may be drawn to the same nurturing, comforting, and caring attributes in you that his mother has. But he is not looking to marry his mother. He doesn't want you treating him like he's your child. I think some women get this part of the "motherly" quality twisted, as some enjoy emasculating their men. Those women are the opposite of what men want and need in a wife.

Women are quite intuitive. They come with uncanny gifts like extra sensory perception and innate, investigative reporter skills. However, women err when they think they know it all. Just as relationships can go bad when one party is taking more than the other, they also go bad when one is talking more than the other.

When a man takes your hand in marriage, he must feel he is being heard as much as you wish to be heard. During a conversation, he may not be very vocal. But when he actually has something to say, you need to listen. You should be tuned in to him as much as you expect him to be tuned in to you. Take advantage of the times he voluntarily shares with you, as this is his way of "opening up." Relish it. He is letting you in past his hardened exterior. Disregard it, and he will shut down and lock you out forever. Just because men don't show emotions often doesn't mean they are devoid of them. Men just find other ways of venting or expressing them. Only those he trusts get to see his transparency.

As the relationship develops, you will have differences of opinion. Allow that man to express his, as you may gain some clarity in the way he views life in general. Don't tell him what he thinks; let him express to you what he thinks and feels. I promise you, your assumptions about a man's thought process or mindset are likely to be wrong. Remember, men and women just don't think the same because we are wired totally differently. So, never try to gauge his responses by what yours would be. Let him share them with you. It's not your job to speak for him.

Ladies, you have the potential to be both wife and mother. You must know which approach to use--and which not to use--with a grown man. Men want to be respected and treated as men. Anything you do that makes him feel like your child, such as correcting or chastising him, will surely lead to an explosive fight. Combat is a man's fun zone, so being combative is always a losing proposition for you. If the "mothering" persists, your beau will decide this isn't the way he wishes to spend the rest of his life. And, this is how infidelity begins.

Don't browbeat your man, even if he is dead wrong. He takes serious offense at this as you are emasculating him. It's even worse if you do it in front of a live audience. Speak to him in private about important matters. Never accuse him unless you have die-hard facts. He will lie to protect both your feelings and his interests. He will also lie to avoid a potential fight.

If you want a more honest man, be a less confrontational woman. You want him to feel he can speak openly on sensitive matters without the fear of starting World War III. I use the word *fear*, but make no mistake about it; that man is far from afraid. He isn't a child. His only fear is that a fight will ensue, ruining any possibility that he will get laid and have a peaceful night. He knows that when you are pissed, there will be no loving; and that man wants his loving.

If you approach your man the wrong way, he will probably overreact. His frustration comes from knowing it will be a few days before you calm down, and the love is back to normal. It also comes from you treating him as your subordinate instead of your husband. If you have an issue, never become mother-like toward him. He will instantly swell up to not feel like the boy who used to have to take that. He is grown now and demands respect as all men do. Give it, and there is a better chance he will be more open and honest.

You want your man to feel you are his best friend, his limitless support system, and his freak in the sheets. When you work these three things, you won't have to wonder if he's taking you seriously; you will see the results. Actions are much louder than words, and men are not that big on words anyway. So, don't take it personally if he isn't as verbally expressive with his appreciation for you. Men show their love and attentiveness in different ways. The key word here is "DIFFERENT."

Ladies, I know it seems that a lot is on you. And it is. Your man is a hardhead, so you have to show him he is safe with you without coming off like his mother. He is not always as emotionally open as you, so teach him without condescension, insult, or aggression. The calmer you appear, the more information he will freely give. And if you want to tell him how you feel about what he shares, keep it conversational. Don't demean him or respond in a dogmatic way. You will have a greater chance of making him feel he can trust you with his whole heart.

I want to see you win. Be loving and patient if you want to get your man to open up to you and stay open. Mothering, nagging, and complaining on the regular will annoy him, causing him to draw back from being honest with you. Instead of telling you what you need to know, he will tell you what you want to hear. This is what men do to keep the peace while remaining safely detached in the relationship. You don't want him to be detached; you want him to feel close to you. This is done with time, love, mutual trust, and support. Create a space that he feels is a safe-haven for truth.

We like the simple things you women do, like when you get a manicure or pedicure, when you keep your hair on fleek, and when you dress nice. We hate when you badger, debate, complain and command. There is a way to get what you want from your man, but it doesn't come from telling him what he must do. That's what mothers do, not his beloved wife.

Chapter Twenty-Eight

SEX IS NOT A WEAPON

Men are very sexual creatures, both the good man and the bad boy. For men, sex is the tie that binds. If the sex is good, he will consider building a serious relationship with you. This is a major component of what he needs to stay interested in you long-term. But, if you want to keep his attention, never use sex as a weapon.

Women sometimes act as if sex isn't important to them when men know it is. Power is also important to some women in relationships. This is why they shut down the sex when they want to. To me, it seems like women think sex gives them a position of control, which also gives them an advantage. Newsflash: It doesn't! When you start using sex as a weapon, you are working against your own relationship's development and progress.

Sex is a major non-negotiable in a man's world. When you start withholding it, he knows it's just a power move. This will quickly put you in a place of conflict. Stay in this place too long, and you are working against your objective of making this man want to marry you or stay married to you. Keep in mind what I've said repeatedly: Most men aren't looking for wives; most are happy dating you without making a heavy commitment. You are the ones who want more, seek more, and demand more. So, you also need to DO more.

Sexual attraction is powerful. The more game a man spits, the more interested a woman becomes in bedding him. That's until he says something stupid to make her see him in the "friend" zone. What's funny is that men have no clue that they may already be in her favor. The inner hunter thinks he is hunting prey he can't see he has already caught. She will have already allowed him to hunt and catch her as soon as she knows he was someone of interest.

Keep it hot in the bedroom and never get lazy in this department. Satisfy his carnal pleasures. Metaphorically speaking, the commitment to have sex with you for life is like promising to eat the same meal three times a day forever. He may love steak, but some occasional lobster, chicken, red beans, jambalaya, crawfish, crabs, pork chops and bacon are also of interest to him. If you wish for him to be like a dog and only eat one food for the rest of his life, that food best be amazing.

To keep things spicy, send him a random sexy picture. Flirt with him like you used to. Surprise him with a bubble bath, candles and those cute things you used to wear so he will know these things still matter to you. Engage sexually before he starts seeking another variety of meal.

Don't use sex in a negative way unless you want long-term negative results. Don't make your man smile in your face while sleeping with another woman behind your back to protect himself from your power moves. Sex is the most beautiful way for people in love to express their care for each other. Use this tool to relax his mind for that uncomfortable conversation you'd like to have. You want him to hear you? Talk to him after he is pleased. You will find him far more receptive to your concerns.

Men hate when they are knee-deep in some sexual flirting, and you stop to remind him you are more than just sex. Save that for when you aren't engaged in a physical encounter. Don't assume he can't see past your body just because the current interaction is highly physical. Don't stop sex talk cold just to make sure he knows you have a brain. He knows you do; that's one of the reasons why he chose you. It's just not an appropriate topic of conversation for that specific moment. He has plenty of time to further explore your wit and interests. Don't stop the flow of conversations he likes, and he won't stop the flow of the ones you like. Remember the importance of give and take.

Using sex as a weapon could work against you, not for you. You might not get any of the results you expect. Instead of a man giving in to your demands, your demands can be ignored, and he will just go get it from someone else. And if you are with a bad boy, he may even take it a step further, and get it from your friend. This is a man's way of saying, "Stop playing games with my time." For you ladies, it's about being in control and getting your way. To the man, it's about frustration and a set-up for deception and cheating.

Withholding sex usually isn't really even about sex per se'.

Starving him sexually may be your effort to draw his attention to a totally unrelated matter. Men know this, but if you do it long enough, he will start seeing other women. Whatever happened to just telling him what you want, or what's really wrong? Withholding sex is not a good practice if you have a good relationship you wish to keep. Sexual intimacy is real and serious for men and playing with it won't make him want you more. He will simply get back into hunter mode, pursue new prey, and deal with you when you are over it. Then again, maybe he won't.

If you want something from your man, but he doesn't respond at first, try another tactic besides withholding sex. Keep things pleasant. Taking away the sex is not the answer. You can get more out of a man with honey than with vinegar. There are other ways to get what you want from him, especially if he is happy.

Sex is a mutual exchange, and it is power. How you use this power will determine how well your relationship works and how long it lasts. Use it correctly, and you can get him to do whatever you want. Use it incorrectly, and you will end up creating a cheating, lying boyfriend who will never be a committed husband for you.

I know some women reading this are probably thinking, *"That right there is some bullshit."* But could that be the reason that you are lonely this very moment? Doing the same thing and expecting a different result is the very definition of *insanity*. Ladies, I'm trying to show you what works and what doesn't from a man's perspective. If your methods haven't successfully landed you a husband, it may be time to try something different.

Life is too short to be unhappy because you've always used manipulative tools, like withholding sex, to get what you want from your man. If you insist on using these tools, you must use them for good. In this case, a little manipulation is fine. Giving him good sex to get your way means that, in the process, he also gets his way. It's a win-win proposition. However, it's horrible if you use sex to piss him off or as punishment because you are unhappy about something. Communication would be a much more effective tool, and it will bring you closer. Don't use sex against him to get his attention. Save sex for love, not revenge.

Chapter Twenty-Nine

KNOW WHEN TO SHUT UP

Here is another one of those fun chapters that tickles the ladies. Yes, there is a point you reach in every fight when what I'm about to tell you is sane, solid advice. So, listen up!

I've already told you that men are naturally combative. Yet, there are some women who love riling men up just to see them express some emotion. But the one emotion that runs through a man very easily during an argument is *aggression*. You may want them to be more sensitive, but many men find it difficult being anything other than the way they were taught so they don't appear weak.

Some women who need attention tend to piss the man off just to get a rise out of him. I have personally dated women and have female friends who believe that a man who shows his feelings-- whatever those feelings are-- is showing them love. They will take negative attention over no attention at all. When he is very upset, he is too distracted to even respond to his text messages or phone calls because the conflict at hand has his undivided focus. Eventually, this will cause a man to blow up; but needy women thrive on attention, even when it is toxic. They enjoy having a man 100 percent focused on them, even if only for a moment and for all the wrong reasons.

Ladies, there's something you need to understand about a man: In every fight, he has the potential of hitting a breaking point. You can avoid letting him reach that point by knowing when it's time to SHUT UP. Sure, his angry expressions may look like passion to you, but I assure you that if he is pushed too far, he will reach the point of combustion. You need not push him to this extreme just to get on his radar.

Since a man is raised from childhood to be defensive and aggressive, provoking him with your words can sometimes cause him to become dangerously enraged. We are talking about destructive levels, now. Breaking things, calling you disrespectful names, and degrading you can be indications that you've pushed him too far. Learn when to shut up, before he starts to hate you. Over time, he will realize you are just provoking him on purpose for selfish reasons and will eventually decide to move on.

Upsetting a man is not the way to get to his emotional core. You must make him feel comfortable expressing himself to you without anger. Men really don't like to be violently angry with their women as it reminds them of male-on-male confrontations. But, if you upset him enough, he will feel challenged as if by another man and will react accordingly. Don't let your mouth make him become that delusional.

I totally agree that a man should never put his hands on a

woman. However, some women persist in agitating men, not realizing they are pushing emotional triggers. Those triggers send men into violence mode. I know women who get all in the man's face yelling, screaming, cussing, spitting at him, chest bumping him, practically goading him into a fight, all to create a scene. These are the same triggers that men push with each other.

If you become aggressive during arguments with your man and he blacks out, strikes you with verbal disrespect, or even with his hands, you now know why it happened. You activated defense mechanisms buried deep inside of him that stem from childhood. Those mechanisms made him aggressive and defensive back then and will cause the same reaction now. You really don't want to be confrontational with a man to the point of forcing him into a dark place just to get his attention and supposedly feel "loved." This is not the way to gauge his love for you, nor are these the emotions you want to make a habit of seeing in your relationship. It may make you feel loved, but it makes him feel something totally different.

A loving, caring woman can earn a man's confidence and trust, thereby enabling him to express more sensitive emotions while in her presence even if he's tough around everyone else. This is what I mean when I say you have to put in some work, ladies. You need to show this man it's okay to reveal a softer side without feeling judged by you.

Ladies, stay classy and don't resort to the worst possible route just to make your man pay attention to you. If he isn't spending enough time with you, change how you communicate with him. You may get excited seeing him lose it, but in time, you will lose him because no man wants an aggravating life partner. I don't care how good the sex is, a man won't tolerate an adversarial mate. He doesn't want a woman who constantly challenges him and doesn't know when to concede. Know when to shut up.

Like a potential alcoholic, you must know when to say "enough" in arguments, especially those you initiate. Even the nicest of men have a breaking point, so be mindful of how far you push him into a corner. Eventually, he could come out swinging. Stay away from stimulations that remind him of male-on-male confrontation, because when upset, he no longer sees you as his woman. Instead, he sees an opponent who is pushing him into a fight, whether a verbal joust or a physical one.

Take the hint when your man seems to be putting his foot down during an argument with you. Take it as your final warning that he is on the brink of exploding. This is not what you want your man to display on a regular basis, because this is not love. Listen, the only time a man will use rage to show his passion for you is when he is protecting you or defending your name or honor. In that instance, he is showing his love for you. It's totally different from when you are the one stirring his rage.

You don't gain respect from your man by being a bitch. He has enough outside pressure beating him down. He doesn't need you beating him down at home. If you disrespect him to the point that he doesn't think you care about his feelings, he will stomp on yours. You may have to call either friends or the police, depending on how deeply you have drawn him into combat. Use restraint and choose your words carefully; you won't lose the fight. Instead, you'll avoid the extreme of where the next moment could go. And that can save your relationship.

When a man reaches that state of anger toward you, it is counter-productive to try building a lasting relationship. He is mad enough at the world as it is; don't make yourself the center of his anger or aggression. When a man tells you it's enough, just shut up. You won't seem weak; you will seem wise. You haven't lost the fight; you will have just picked your battles better. There's no need for either to win petty points. Wait until calmer heads prevail, then you can revisit your issue. I promise you, tomorrow when he is calmer, he will HEAR you, and that's when you can let him have it, if you like. He is in a state of HEARING you now.

The point here is that not fueling the fire doesn't mean you are losing the fight. You are winning. You just need to let him simmer; he will be ready to hear you. Stick to your objective of being heard, not winning a useless fight. Pride down, your time is coming to make your point successfully.

I will say it until I am blue in the face: If you wish to be someone's wife, getting there is based on what you present and project. A man is not going to see you as a potential wife by proxy just because you gave him some ass. You must show him you are a long-term proposition, not a temporary one. How you handle conflict and how well you use restraint during disagreements will hold relevance when he's deciding if you will or won't be his life partner.

Ladies, the power you have is real. To the same extent that you can push a man to extreme anger, you can comfort him at his lowest points. I cannot express enough how this one element can mean life or death for your relationship.

Chapter Thirty

BE HIS BIGGEST MOTIVATOR

Being your man's biggest motivator is key to locking him down. A man wants a mate that not only believes in his dreams, but actively participates in making them happen for him. This will ultimately benefit you both.

My wife is a perfect example of this. As I shared earlier, she positioned me to be noticed by a major talent agent by simply keeping my photo on her reception desk until someone eventually asked who I was. That got me my first interview. Eventually, I would go on to do every type of voice job from commercials, to cartoons, to movies, and TV promotions. For 8 years, I was the voice of the UPN Network, promoting every show from *"Homeboys in Outer Space"* to *"Girlfriends."*

To keep my career moving, she became both my publicist and my manager, handling my contracts, independent films, and appearances. She became a big part of the machine that was my brand, and it was her participation that kept her at the forefront of my life.

Think about it. Outside of you, what else is a man's passion? It's his career choice. I said "choice" because, unless it's really his choice versus something he's obligated to do, it isn't necessarily his passion. More than likely, his career is something he was working on before he met you. It's been his top priority and how he's spent most of his time. If you are involved in this area of his life, you increase your value in terms of being viewed as a life-long mate. Just as you wish for him to be all into you, he desires you to be all into him. Participate in the building of the dynasty that makes him see you as a part of the empire, the first lady of the "Power Couple."

    A woman who helps her man build his dreams becomes equally as important as the dream itself. A man loves a woman who is into his goals. This is actually a win-win situation for both because now she adds business time into their personal time which means a lot more time together. They are collaborating to build a dream, and teamwork makes the dream work. Find a way to participate in his money-making endeavors and become an asset, not a liability. Tell him he is doing a great job and be his number one cheerleader.

    The worst thing you can do to a man with great ambition is be a nag. It's a huge turn-off and the quickest way to reduce yourself to a passing fling, or a side-chick. He may not say anything to you, but you will surely be repositioned out of the future "wife" category, and into the part-time "ass" category. Sure, he will continue to sleep with you, but he will have already concluded that you will be more problematic than beneficial to his future. A man's career is very important to him. Your interference with his aspirations adds to his daily struggle and the stress he encounters while trying to become successful.

Some men's careers have no room, space, or need for anything from you past love and emotional support. Men in service professions (police officers or firemen, for example) only need your support as they go out and risk their lives daily for the safety of the public. There are also men who may not want or need you in their business circles. They only require knowing that you are in their corner, something you will easily convey when your support is genuine.

Again, self-assess and be real about what you can handle in a husband. If you know you are the kind of woman who needs a lot of interaction on a regular basis, marry a man who can give it. Never expect more out of a man than he can do without being pressured. To do so will keep you dissatisfied with the relationship.

A man looks for a woman who is supportive, motivating, and encouraging. Those three things will make him feel the need to go the distance with you and forget all other women. Think about that for a minute. You want him to forget all other women, including all of those sexy ladies who can provide him with a variety of titillating experiences. You want him to walk away forever from all those opportunities. Just know that the more popular your man is, the more options he has. And those options continually present themselves, even after marriage.

There are women who believe in karma, so they won't dare touch a married man. But some will pursue him because a man who can commit is highly attractive. A true alpha male will still draw the attention of masses of women whether he is married or not. That's why you must hold his interest long after he says, "I do."

I've been married for 26 years, and titties and ass still fall out of my cell phone and inbox on Facebook to this day. Some single women are skilled in the art of competing to win a married man from his wife. If you leave even a crack in the door, a man with so many options may one day decide to take up one of them, or even two. Allowing a lapse in your relationship affords another woman the opportunity to prove that she may be a better choice for him.

I can tell you firsthand I have many options in the event my wife chooses to walk away. She is well aware of this fact, knowing she is married to an entertainer. My case is special because, in movies, I'm known for portraying the very types of men that draw women like a moth to a flame. Even at my age, women half of 50 will send me pictures and offer themselves to me for both business and pleasure. For a man with options, jealousy is a quality that is frowned upon. You must know and accept that this comes with the territory for men like myself; so give him reasons to want to rush home only to you. You have the power, ladies. My wife knows her power and is unfazed by the attention my celebrity brings.

If you have a celebrity man and tend to be jealous, change the way you view things. You have a man that everyone wants. Instead of being jealous, revel in it. He chose you. He could have all these other women of different shapes, sizes, ages and walks of life; but he chose you. You should want a man that other women want; you want someone desirable, don't you?

The way you choose to view the situation and your reaction to his popularity determines where your relationship with him will go. You must table your insecurities and remember that he chose YOU. With all the attention he gets, he still wants YOUR support and praise, as it will mean more to him than when he gets it from anyone else.

A smart woman will learn how to keep her man motivated. She pays close attention to what gives him energy. At times, he will fall and have trouble understanding why, causing him to not quickly bounce back. Defeat is hard on a man, as failure is not really an option in his world. The woman who can pick up his spirit and push him forward is the woman he wants for life.

A woman that represents a support system is far more attractive to a man than one who always draw attention to herself. He doesn't like a woman who makes herself, her feelings, and her need for attention her biggest priority. In all likelihood, he will eventually hurt her, first by cheating, and then by leaving altogether. Or, at worst, he may intentionally break her heart, forcing her to leave him just to protect himself.

Building up your man is crucial. It's not what a woman makes a man feel about her, but what a woman makes a man feel about *himself* that grabs his heart. When he sees a woman who can handle life not being always about her 24/7, he will start to see what separates her from the rest who are vying for his attention. That's the woman he will want to spend most of his time with. Be mindful, you want a husband, not a boyfriend. Once you find a man who you believe qualifies as a mate, don't try to change him. Accept and enhance him.

A man determines if a woman is to be his wife when he sees where she stands when he is at his lowest points in life. I've talked to many men, and I can say that we've all been in a lonely place, even when there are people all around us. We refer to it as a "dark place" where we are at our lowest emotionally. It's the abyss of darkness when even the strongest man has pain he can't control or explain. That feeling is often triggered by the loss of someone close like a parent or sibling, or when your career suffers turmoil after being passed up for a desired position, or when a business plan fails. When a man falls into this dark place, he learns quickly what his woman is made of.

Ladies, how you treat a man at his lowest point will determine how far he takes you into his life. No man wants a fair-weather wife. He wants that "ride or die" woman who will stick with him through thick and thin. Any woman can love on a man when he is on top, feeling good, and winning in life. His soul mate will be the one who rides with him when he is on the ground. She is the one who scrapes him up and puts him back together.

You say you want a man who will open up to you. The biggest opening you will ever have to a man's emotions will be the time when he experiences failure. He will literally crumble like dust when he feels the world is against him, and his efforts are thwarted. This vulnerable man is seeking someone who still sees him, his dreams, and his value, even when he feels all else have turned their backs. The woman who neglects to answer his failure with her encouragement will never get a second chance.

When a man is most vulnerable, he needs to see strength from his wife or would-be mate. The woman that passes this test is the one he will always want to take care of and spend his good times with once they return. Life comes chock full of problems that affect the homestead, and a man needs a woman who knows how to motivate him back on his path when life sends him too many detours. You can be that woman if you refrain from kicking him when he is already down, as doing so will only make him hate you in the end.

Ladies, you have powerful input into a man's life. As a wife, you will have to be at the forefront as your husband's positive reinforcement. You can propel him forward in his ambitions and dreams. However, if you don't, another woman will gladly do your job. And you shouldn't get mad at her. She has no allegiance to you. She just sees a man with whom she wants to build a life and is willing to stand tough behind him. She may be a thorn in your side, but to him, she is a breath of fresh air, and will do what he really wants YOU to do without always having to ask you. You can call this other woman a whore, a home wrecker, or a THOT, but she's just a woman who wants your man in her future. She is not playing games; she is COMPETING.

Now, unless this other woman is a friend, past or present,

your beef is not with her; it is with your mate. If he is straying, you, dear, may have something to do with that. Your attitude toward him when he was at his lowest may have opened the door. Understand that failing to support him when he is down is the surest way to lose his heart and trust forever. He sees with greatest clarity when he is at his lowest. That's when he gets an unobstructed view of who his lover, true friends, business associates, and family members really are. I promise you, he will never forget those who stepped on him when life sank, especially his family and his woman, because he expects their support to be steadfast.

Ladies, be your man's rock at all times. Show him your worth by reaffirming his worth. A woman who supports and motivates her man will surely be his wife, if she isn't already. Be his shoulder to cry on, and you will indeed see him become unguarded enough to cry. That's how you can get him to feel comfortable being emotional in your presence. This is what all men want and need.

I've dated women who saw something happen to me that brought me down, and they just disappeared! No love, no support, didn't even check on a brother. They saw me in a funk, and instead of having my back in my time of need, they got as far away from me as possible. These were fair-weather women, who will have never been anything more than a roll in the sheets. Literally. They made it as clear as the nose on my face that they were too selfish to let my pain matter to them, even a little.

A man cannot tolerate any woman who is self-absorbed,

negligent, and insecure. Lose these bad qualities fast if you want to be considered wife material.

Chapter Thirty-One

ACCOUNTABILITY IS RESPONSIBILITY

Another issue that stifles growth in relationships is *uneven accountability*. A good woman can encourage a man to be accountable for his actions. Conversely, a man wants a woman who is accountable for hers.

I've dated countless women who were very masterful at holding me accountable for every negative deed but refused to hold themselves to the same standard. A good example of this is a woman that I once dated who fell on hard times several years ago. I was there for her when she lost her home. In addition to helping her pack all her belongings, I slept in the car with her until the next day because she didn't have a truck to move her things from in front of the house. At her lowest, I was there in full support, when I could have been home, or working on my career. However, this very same woman later stopped being my friend because, one day, I was depressed.

Now, anyone who has ever dealt with depression knows that when a person is to the point of feeling suicidal, you don't turn your back on him, as he is in a dark and dangerous mental space, right? Well, this woman showed concern that one night, but never called again to check on me. When I called her out on it, she just stopped speaking to me altogether. She preferred leaving than to be held accountable for her negligence.

It would have been mature and responsible of her to simply own up to the fact that she was remiss, apologize, and make things right. After all, hadn't I been there for her when she was in dire straits? Had I just abandoned her, I would've expected her to call me out on it. This is what two people in a relationship are supposed to do to keep it together.

This same woman could very specifically recount every single one of my offensive words or deeds in fine detail. But when it was time for her to own her own bullshit, she denied it all, defended it all, and justified it all. When I asked her to think specifically about what she did wrong, her response was always generalized with broad strokes like, *"I know I got issues."* Of course, I always asked her to be more specific. She was NEVER specific about her negligent and offensive behavior but was so on point when I did something that affected her. Clearly, she had the ability to differentiate between right and wrong, but only when wrong was done to her, not when she was the offender. That's very messed up.

This is the mark of a selfish person, and no man wants a selfish mate. Period. When you demand accountability from a man, you should be just as willing to be accountable to him. A man respects you when you own your failures, change your behavior, and try to make things work. He will neither respect nor like you if your words never match your actions. You will create an enemy out of a lover and friend. Love is the opposite of selfishness.

In marriage, both parties will make mistakes. Both are human. But how you recover from those mistakes determines the value of your relationship. This woman clearly didn't value my time, my dreams, or my aspirations. Consequently, the relationship was destined to die. All I got was a bunch of right words with opposite actions. She would rather leave than take responsibility.

If you want a real relationship, understand that you will have to hold yourself accountable for what you do, or don't do. If accountability seems to escape you every time you're confronted about your actions, stay single because that won't work in marriage. Go ahead and focus on your needs and don't waste a man's time talking marriage stuff because you are not marriage worthy. Stock up on D batteries, or accept you are nothing more to a man than an overnighter, as a husband expects more of a wife.

Being self-centered, you will probably never have anything good to say about men anyway, because honestly, they will just want to hit it, quit it, and never commit to it. You provide them no vision of a real future with you. And keep in mind that those same men are hitting and quitting other women just like you. What they won't quit is a woman mature enough to own her stuff, one who knows how to apologize, and knows how to forgive when she receives an apology.

Ladies, no man is going to stand outside your life and be your cheerleader. Either you will both be in the game, or you won't. You are not going to find a husband being half-ass because he is looking for a woman who is about 100% participation in making love work and the relationship last. If you don't want to fully participate in a relationship, don't ask any man to take you seriously; just enjoy the dick. That's all it will ever be for a woman who won't be accountable for her actions.

Chapter Thirty-Two

IF YOU DON'T HAVE TIME, DON'T HAVE A RELATIONSHIP

TIME is essential to the survival of any real relationship. A man wants a woman who is attentive and makes time to grow together with him regardless of her busy schedule. *"You aren't worth it"* is the message he gets when everything else in her life takes precedence over him. He can't build anything meaningful with a woman who is always making excuses about her unavailability as he watches her save the rest of the world. He wants someone who looks forward to spending QUALITY time with him. He doesn't want to have to beg, or repeatedly argue over this issue.

You can't be the type of woman who will deal with him only on your terms. If you won't lay everything else aside just to devote attention to your man, don't be surprised when he gets it elsewhere. Negligent women are often shocked when they find they've been reduced to side-chick status without notice, versus being viewed as a potential wife. Sadly, they seldom see it coming.

I know that compromise for some of you can be difficult.

But a man won't stay with you very long if you can't be flexible. You must have good time management skills and be able to bend some if your desire is to have something that will lead to marriage. Furthermore, the way you value a man's time will determine just how much of it you're worthy of having. When it's misused or treated with disrespect, you risk creating a lot of conflict between you and your man.

You can't let your life cause you to be so busy with everything and everyone else and expect him to put his life on hold until yours thins out. Cut your losses and move on before it gets too serious. Don't let him waste his precious hours and minutes on what will end up being a tumultuous relationship.

Your man has other things in his life aside from you. He has his career, his hobbies, his family, and his friends. He also has other women eyeballing him, waiting for you to slip up. If you only want to be bothered with him at your convenience, you will end up with a cheater. Giving him so much free time will allow other women opportunity to step up and give him all the attention he needs without him having to ask. If your commitment to the relationship goes beyond just words, however, he won't be as tempted to step out on you. It's your call. Either make him a priority or be ready to deal with the consequences.

It bears repeating: A man's needs are just as important as yours. He will notice if the relationship is lopsided with your needs always on the forefront, while his suffer on the backburner. Instead of breaking up with you, he will simply cheat on you until you find time for him. This is how a man seeks revenge when his needs are overlooked. And if you really piss him off, he will cheat with someone you know. So, when your girlfriend ends up pregnant by your man, this was his way of showing you someone else valued him more than you.

I know quite a few women who despise their men for fathering kids with their close friends. But when you neither respect your man nor regard his feelings, he will want to get revenge by hurting you. There are millions of women he can bed, but deliberately seducing your close friend with whom you've shared your business tends to sting you that much more. A man's catch-back game is savage when you start playing with his emotions. Granted, some men do messed up shit to you just because they are messed up men. In many cases, however, they are paying you back for wasting their time.

Many things, once lost, can be found again. You can lose money, for example, but can always get more, even if it takes a while. But ladies, once time is lost, you don't get it back. For this reason, TIME is very important to a man. He will invest so much into you, but in return, he expects your time and attention beyond just sex. If you are still single, but don't have time to build the relationship, he knows that you won't have time for a marriage either. That means he is unlikely to choose you as his wife. He will go back to playing the field where he can find a woman whose schedule is more flexible than yours.

Stop right now and think about it. Are you prioritizing other things over your relationship? The time you neglect to give to your man allows him the opportunity to deeply bond with someone else. Honestly, you have no room to be mad or feel betrayed when you give him plenty of space to develop intimacy with another woman. YOU are the one who will have done that. You shouldn't put him in the position of having to press you to be with him. You should see the value of his presence in your life and believe in him enough to invest your presence in his and his dreams. Don't let another woman function as the "Mrs." in his world.

Ladies, if you know that you have consistently dismissed your man and his needs, don't wait until he leaves you cold to acknowledge the impact of your behavior. Don't start the "blame game" by focusing all attention on what he did or didn't do. First, do some self-assessment, carefully considering your lack of participation in his life. Women who remain in denial and refuse to face their flaws end up alone their entire lives. A man has very little tolerance for a woman who won't own her stuff. You must be clear about the mess you create by being honest and willing to change if you want to be someone's wife.

Chapter Thirty-Three

EXCUSES ARE USELESS

When I pledged Omega Psi Phi Fraternity, Inc. in 1985, one of the things they emphasized was the futility of EXCUSES. We often heard reminders that went something like this: "Excuses are monuments of nothing. They build bridges to nowhere. Those who use these tools are incompetent and masters of nothingness." I have held true to this wisdom since that time and have seen its positive impact on my life for decades.

People who are always making excuses are difficult to partner with, especially in a marriage. They spend more energy justifying why they can't do something instead of simply DOING it. The time it takes to weasel out of promises could be spent on making those promises good. They have a bad habit of creating believable justifications to back their reasons for failing to follow through. When this becomes a persistent pattern, precious time is wasted, and trust is lost.

If you are serious about moving forward with your man, you will heed the advice I'm about to share, especially if you want him to be fully committed to you. When you live in truth, there are no reasons to lie or to make excuses. Just as you hate liars, so do men. Your actions are what really count, so let them do the talking for you.

A man will regard what you *do* more than what you *say*. When you repeatedly deliver lame excuses, he will lose interest in you and pursue the woman whose promises can be trusted. You will think, *"Everything was great, then he turned around and asked some other bitch to marry him."* You THOUGHT everything was great. Your carelessness will have allowed your man to develop a full, meaningful bond with another woman who is serious about him, fills that free time you left vacant, and follows through without making excuses. She will have gotten the message you failed to get. You can't get mad at either of them. You will have had a chance to do the same.

Chapter Thirty-Four

THE FIRST DAY OF THE REST OF YOUR LIFE

Congratulations, Ladies! You made it through this book. You've heard some hard truths and learned some tough lessons, but you stuck it out. My hope is that you are encouraged, knowing that, regardless of your past, love and marriage are real possibilities for you. I've given you the male perspective and I've equipped you with practical information. Now, you know what to do. I'm confident that, if applied, the wisdom shared here will improve your chances of becoming some lucky man's wife. You deserve it.

Marriage is a beautiful thing. It thrives on relentless, unconditional love, trust, commitment, dedication, and pleasure. It's a bond between two imperfect people who pledge to have each other's backs through tragedy and triumph, in sickness and in health, for better or for worse, for richer or for poorer. It's a covenant that requires 100% buy-in from both husband and wife. Marriage is also a thankless, checkless job; a real exercise in tolerance and patience. It's not some dream or fairy-tale that casts you in the role of perpetual "bride." Instead, it is hard work that requires your daily commitment and perseverance. With practical wisdom, preparation, and determination, marriage can be a wonderful, fruitful adventure.

Ladies, if you know that marriage is for you, you are now equipped to become a wife. If marriage isn't for you, that's okay too. There's nothing wrong with choosing to remain single. Live true to yourself and be honest with the men you date. Always make your intentions for your relationships clear. And if at any point you decide you want to be married, you now know how to change your behavior and be the woman who can show the right man why he should select you.

I thank God for my wife, Jennifer, who sees me past my flaws and loves me still. And even with her shortcomings, she has never been unreal or dishonest. Makeup can be applied and removed. Weight can be gained and lost. Money comes and goes. But character is constant.

Each in her own way, both Bella and Angel made me a better husband by helping me to see, with crystal clarity, the true value of my wife. And, as she has done for the past 26 years, Jennifer continues to make me both a better man and a better all-around human being. After all these years, I couldn't be happier to have ridden the waves of marriage with such a great woman. We have a solid foundation, a shared understanding, and an openness with each other for which I am deeply grateful. I look forward to us spending many more years together.

Ladies, you must marry for the RIGHT reasons. Love unconditionally and relentlessly. Be in true partnership with your mate. Show him that nothing is more important to you than his happiness. Take care of each other's needs on all levels. Trust each other. Work out your differences with love. Have more fun with each other than with anyone else.

Finally, when he asks for your hand, drop me a line. I'd like to hear your story. Nothing would give me greater joy than to learn why he married you. Love never fails.

"Ladies, remember your bjective."

-Gary Anthony Sturgis

For more information about this book and future publications, or to contact Gary Anthony Sturgis for appearances, contact him via e-mail:

Crescent City Publishing

whyhewont@gmail.com

For book signings and live chat dates for book discussions, visit us at:
www.whyhewontmarry.com

Crescent City Publishing--Los Angeles, CA

www.ingramcontent.com/pod-product-compliance
Lightning Source LLC
Chambersburg PA
CBHW070740160426
43192CB00009B/1513